ANIMALS MAKE YOU FEEL BETTER

ANIMALS MAKE YOU FEEL BETTER

Real life stories of how pets and wild animals have helped their human friends

JOHN G. SUTTON

Illustrated by Elizabeth Kay

*This book is dedicated to the memory of
my late father, Frank Sutton*

All rights reserved. No part of this publication may be reproduced or transmitted by
any means, electronic, mechanical, photocopying or otherwise, without the prior
permission of the publisher.

First published in Great Britain in 1998 by Element Children's Books
Shaftesbury, Dorset SP7 8BP

Published in the USA in 1998 by Element Books Inc.
PO Box Box 830, Boston MA

Published in Australia in 1998 by Element Books Limited
for Penguin Books Australia Ltd, PO Box 257, Victoria 3134

Copyright © Text John G. Sutton 1998
Copyright © Illustrations Elizabeth Kay 1998

The moral rights of the author and illustrator have been asserted.

British Library Cataloguing in Publication data available.
Library of Congress Cataloguing in Publication data available.

ISBN 1 90188 100 8

Cover design by Alison Withey
Cover picture *Telegraph Colour Library*
Text Design by Dorchester Typesetting Group Ltd
Printed and bound in Great Britain by
Biddles Ltd, Guildford and King's Lynn

CONTENTS

ACKNOWLEDGMENTS

The author wishes to acknowledge the help and assistance given to him by the following individuals, organizations, and charitable institutions:

Ms. Helen Cottington of the Camomile Centre, Lower Bowden Farm, Firzeleigh Lane, Bovey Tracey, South Devon TQ13 9LX, UK;

Professor Dr. Horace Dobbs of International Dolphin Watch, North Ferriby, Humberside HU14 3ET, UK;

Dr. Elisabeth Svendsen MBE of the Elisabeth Svendsen Trust for Children and Donkeys, Sidmouth, Devon EX10 0NU, UK;

Mr. Philip Stott of the North West Office of Guide Dogs for the Blind, Nuffield House, Lowndes Street, Bolton BL1 4QA, UK;

Dr. Anthony Podberscek, BVSc, PhD, of the Animal Welfare and Human-Animal Interactions Group at the Department of Clinical Veterinary Medicine, University of Cambridge, UK, who supplied the information for and kindly read the first chapter on What the Scientists Say;

Mr. Vincent Hogan, Managing Director, Our Dogs Publishing, Station Approaches, Manchester, UK;

Mrs. Lois J. Barin, MA, Ohio State University, Columbus, Ohio, USA;

Mrs. Dorothy Bannister, Leyland, Preston, Lancashire, UK;

Ms. Jennifer Smith of the Education Office, National Canine Defence League, 17 Wakely Street, London EC1V 7LT;

Mr. Paul Teasdale of the International League for the Protection of Horses, Anne Colvin House, Snetterton, Norwich, Norfolk NR16 2LR.

INTRODUCTION

Animals really do make me feel better. As the author of this book you would expect me to say that, but it's true. Let me give you an example. On my forty-seventh birthday I was sitting alone in my home looking at the one card I had received. My wife was the only person who had remembered. For a few lonely moments I felt really sad, as though all the friends I thought I had didn't care at all. They had forgotten me on my special day.

Then up walked Grumbles, my British bulldog, and flopped her big heavy head on my knee. She shuffled it about and stared up at me with her baggy old eyes and, as I gazed into them, I could sense a feeling of pure love coming to me from her. It was as though she were saying, "Come on, John, don't be sad! I'm your friend."

I could have laughed out loud then. Grumbles knew I was feeling sorry for myself and had come to cheer me up. That simple happy experience made me wonder, did Grumbles love me? I knew then I had to write this book to tell others about the simple joy that our friends from the animal kingdom can bring into our lives.

Of course there are serious scientists who will state with authority that animals react to physical stimulation and are not really thinking things through. Yet there are stories in this book that seem to demonstrate that some animals do think and, having thought, act to help their human friends. You will, I hope, form your own opinions.

There are simple tests and assessments at the end of each true story. These have been specially devised to help you consider the options presented within the text.

Perhaps you may be skeptical about the reasons our friends in the animal kingdom act in the way described. You will be invited to make your own mind up about the nature of animal and human interactions. For example, do you believe that our four-legged or feathered friends have feelings or emotions that are similar to ours? Read this book before you answer that one.

John G. Sutton

P.S. I was forty-eight this year and I got two cards this time - Grumbles sent me one!

ANIMALS MAKE PEOPLE FEEL BETTER:
What the Scientists Say

Many different kinds of animal have been kept by people for thousands of years, both as workers and as pets. People take for granted that they benefit from contact with animals. Recently scientists have become interested in how and why this works.

According to one estimate, at least half the households in the Western world have some kind of animal as a pet. Cats and dogs are about equally popular; all the miscellaneous other creatures that people keep as pets, from ponies to stick insects, add up to a small minority. If you own a pet, you may already have an opinion about animals making you feel better. Perhaps you simply enjoy being with your pet, playing and having fun. I know playing with my bulldog Grumbles can cheer me up any day. And it seems that doctors and scientists will back me up on this.

Medical benefits of pets

Cat and dog owners generally live longer and healthier lives than people without pets. Even keeping a bird is better than having just a house plant to talk to, for those who are elderly and live alone, one English study found.

But how could dogs be good for people who have had heart surgery? Well, it has been discovered that when people stroke a dog, their blood pressure drops. High blood pressure can cause a lot of problems for heart-surgery patients, so a friendly dog has a positive healing effect in such cases.

Dogs are also good for patients who have to be in hospital for a long time, perhaps the rest of their lives. A program of regular visits from dogs has been found to make such patients more cheerful, more active, and happier. There are now many organizations that take animals to meet sick people and befriend them.

We all know about seeing-eye dogs, but there is now another special mission for the carers of the dog world. Certain dogs can be trained to warn people suffering from epilepsy of an oncoming fit before it happens. Such seizures can be quite sudden, and cause sufferers to fall down with hardly any warning at all. In some circumstances this can put sufferers in danger: they might burn themselves with a hot iron or drown in the bath. So a dog that can sense a fit in advance might save its owner's life. One explanation of this seemingly magical ability is that these dogs are sensitive to the electric activity within the epileptic sufferer's brain.

Pets help children

Some young people have behavior problems and get into trouble. Dog visits can help them too. Doctors have observed improvement in the behavior of young, emotionally disturbed people when pets were taken to meet them. One therapist noticed that he got the best results after his child patients had made friends with his dog. He went on to base a new method of psychotherapy on this fact.

Several studies suggest that contact with animals helps young people to overcome negative feelings and to value themselves as people. This is because as pet owners they learn to care for animals and behave in a responsible way. For the first time in their lives another living creature depends on them. This can give young people higher self-esteem. The love that they receive from their pets in return for this care also makes them feel good about themselves.

And pets can prevent kids from getting into trouble in the first place. This is because caring for animals helps children to develop their ability to form personal relationships. Children brought up with pet animals are better at playing group games, for example. They are more popular with other children and have more friends. They may have learned important social skills by having fun with their pets. Playing with pets also helps children to develop their imaginations.

Dolphin doctors

It is not just the everyday kind of pet animal that can make human beings feel better. Swimming in the sea with dolphins has become a popular therapy for both mental and physical problems in several parts of the world. For example, there are dolphin swim programmes for disabled young children in Florida. The dolphins have not yet begun to charge for their cooperation.

Horse riding to health

Many benefits are gained by disabled people who enjoy being on a horse, a pony, or even a donkey. As well as being good fun, it improves the rider's physical health in many ways. Balance is improved as the rider learns to sit upright in the saddle and, as a direct result, muscular control develops to some extent. Even people usually confined to a wheelchair benefit from improved self-image by riding. For once in their lives they are looking down on and not up to other people.

These are just some of the facts recently discovered about how and why animals make people feel better. New findings are made all the time. The possibilities are enormous, so stay tuned to your pet!

TROY: The Horse That Saved A Lady

Deep in the green Shropshire countryside, on the out-skirts of Whitchurch, in a manor house overgrown with ivy and vines, there live Lord and Lady Hill. All her life Gina, Lady Hill, has been a keen horsewoman. She learned to ride almost before she could walk. Her husband, the lord of the manor, shares her love of equestrian sport and their stables hold a number of prizewinning show-jumpers.

Not wanted by the police

In 1996 Gina met former Chief Inspector Paul Teasdale, who was previously a member of the mounted police. On his retirement, Paul had been appointed placement officer with the International League for the Protection of Horses, a charitable organization that helps to find homes for retired police horses. They deserve a little peace at the end of a hard working life. Paul knew that good homes are not easy to find, but he had seen Lady Hill's clean stables and thought them ideal. So when he had a horse to place, he at once telephoned the manor house. Would Her Ladyship consider an ex-Birmingham City Police horse? He told her that the gelding was over seventeen hands in height, a dark bay with a white blaze. Gina agreed to look this horse over, and the next week Paul brought it round to her home.

As soon as she sat on top of the big horse, Gina fell in love. There was something very dignified about the way this huge creature held itself, as if it were in command. It was every inch a police horse, with a big chest, a powerful body, mighty legs, and a determined air that seemed to say, "The boss is here." When this impressive horse nuzzled its great soft nose into her face as if asking to be accepted, she could not resist. Paul drove back to Birmingham with an empty horse box.

Gina named the big bay Troy and soon she was riding him through the winding woodland paths that surround her picturesque English home. There, in the shaded glades of Shropshire, where the quiet countryside rolls out to the distant Welsh mountains, they became a team. At first she wondered whether Troy would accept his new role as a rural roustabout, but she need not have worried. Troy just loved the long walks and did not seem to miss the crowded streets of the city. Lord Hill could hardly believe how quickly Troy had made himself at home.

Troy and Lady Hill became the very best of friends. Each day as she entered the stables, Troy would make a whinnying noise as though calling her name. She had many horses to choose from, but the proud bay was now her favorite.

A fateful day

One day in April 1997, Gina decided to ride out with her mother to visit a friend in the nearby village of Hankelow. She saddled up Troy, while her mother Gloria rode a dapple-grey filly called Cadenza. The morning was bright with just a few dark clouds scudding by in the early spring sky. But some miles from the manor house, perhaps halfway to her friend's home, the rain came.

At first there seemed nothing to be concerned about. April showers never hurt anyone, or so she thought. But this was no shower. Swiftly the day darkened as thunder clouds stormed in, chased by the wild west wind. A hard shower of hailstones stung Gina and her mother; then cold sleet soaked them to the skin. They could not continue their journey. In fact, the sooner they were back at the manor house, the better.

It was then that Gina made a terrible error. Thinking they could take a short cut, she led Troy onto the towpath of the Shropshire Union Canal. Still the rain fell, the thunder boomed, and lightning forked out from deep-black clouds. Troy was unmoved by this display of nature's fearsome forces. Behind on Cadenza, Gloria was terrified. Her horse was not trained to ignore loud noises, and clearly hated this dreadful weather. Still, she had the filly under control.

Suddenly Troy lurched to the right as the banking at the side of the canal gave way beneath his weight. Both horse and rider disappeared into the flooded waters.

A life-and-death struggle

Almost in shock, Gloria kept scanning the dark surface of the canal, but for what seemed like minutes, neither horse nor rider was seen. Then Troy's great noble head burst through the mud-clouded waters and he shook it from side to side, creating waves that surged sideways to the bank. But where was Gina?

The horse was struggling now, stuck in the thick mud of the canal bed. Then Gloria saw her daughter, drifting face down in the dirty brown water. At the same time, Troy must have seen his friend. With one tremendous effort he fought free of the mud and heaved his huge body in her direction.

Trembling and terrified, Gloria stared wide-eyed as Troy forced himself through the water toward where his owner lay, floating unconscious on the surface. Her riding hat was split clean in two from the impact of her fall onto the stone banking. Motionless she lay, drifting in midstream, as the roaring storm whipped the cold, dark waters about her. For all Gloria knew, her daughter was dead.

Troy is a hero

From nearby two local farmers came running. They had seen the accident and had got a man on a moored barge to call for the emergency services. But they couldn't reach Lady Hill floating in the middle of the canal.

Then Troy came alongside his friend. Gloria watched in disbelief as the horse ducked its great head under the water and lifted her up. Heaving and pushing, Troy shoved the body of the lady he loved to the side of the embankment. There the two farmers helped pull her clear from the bitterly cold water of the flooded canal. Returning to consciousness, she lay on the towpath, coughing and spluttering, clearing her lungs of the foul water.

Next, the farmers tried to save the horse. But Troy had become trapped by the thick slime that lay on the bottom of the canal. All that could now be seen of this brave creature was his nose poking out from the water, which was rapidly rising as the rain poured down.

Gloria, in tears, held her daughter tight in her arms. As she watched the fast-fading efforts of the horse that had saved Gina's life, she feared that his last courageous deed had been done. Suddenly Troy's head rose above the foul waters. He had fought himself clear of the clinging mud. Splashing and snorting with the effort, the mighty horse clawed his way to the side of the canal. Then, with what little remained of his strength, Troy scrambled up the broken bank and stood on the towpath, alive.

The ultimate sacrifice

Today Lady Hill is certain that without the help of her brave horse Troy she would have drowned. She is amazed that the horse put her safety before his own. In his efforts to shove her out of the water, Troy had pushed himself deep into the slippery mud on the bed of the canal. He must have felt himself sinking into the slime, yet he was prepared to make the ultimate sacrifice for his friend. Lady Hill will never forget that, ever.

— ASSESSMENT —

Q1. Do you believe that Troy could recognize Lady Hill and call her name with a whinny?
a) Horses recognize those who care for them, but do not learn their names.
b) Troy whinnied with excitement when he saw her because it made him hope for a pat, a carrot, or exercise.
c) Troy called to Lady Hill as best he could because knew that she was his friend and he liked her.

Q2. Why do you think Troy pushed Lady Hill to the side of the canal?
a) Struggling to get to the side of the canal, the horse happened to shove her before him.
b) As a police horse, Troy was trained not to leave his rider.
c) Troy saw that his owner was in need of help and he consciously went to her aid.

ALEX and LADY: They Protected a Sick Man

In one of the Southern states of America there lives a man whose life was protected by two pet dogs: Alex, a shih-tzu, and Lady, a large Labrador. Our story starts in the early autumn of 1996, when Al Collier first became poorly. After a collapse, he was diagnosed as having a diseased heart. The doctor told him that the condition might kill him.

Al is a man in great demand. He runs a centre for spiritual development, where friends and clients are always calling round. He is extremely busy with his work and not at all used to taking things easy. But the doctor ordered medication and bed rest.

Dogged nursing

Throughout the six to eight weeks it took Al to recover, the two pet dogs guarded his every movement. They even took it in turns to sit at his bedside. If Alex had to go outside to eat or whatever, he was immediately replaced by Lady. At night both pets slept alongside Al's bed. All those who came close were met by the growls and snarls of these two dogs.

At times both Alex and Lady would join together to prevent Al from getting out of bed. It was as if they knew that he needed rest to get better. Little Alex would jump up on the covers and press his body against Al's, holding him gently in place, while Lady, a much bigger dog, would lie down alongside him with a huge paw on his shoulder and stare into his eyes as if pleading with him to stay still. Al swears he could feel the love those dogs had for him just flooding through him.

On one occasion a woman called who was just a little too demanding. She was a dear friend of long standing and a very good client of Al's centre, so Al told the dogs to let her through. However, despite his instructions, Alex seemed to sense that Al was becoming too tired to continue the meeting. The dog began growling at the woman until she got the message and left Al to rest.

Guardian angels?

The strange thing is that Alex didn't belong to Al at all. The shih-tzu was the pet of his stepson James, and before Al became ill, Alex would have nothing to do with him. It was only during his period of sickness that the shih-tzu came to him.

When Al finally recovered, Alex reverted to his usual

behavior and turned his back on Al. But one day he had undertaken more work than he could handle and had a relapse. Feeling faint and about to collapse, Al staggered upstairs to rest in bed. When he awoke, there were Alex and Lady lying by his side, protecting him.

Al is sure that these pets are his guardian angels in disguise. They certainly seem to know when he is in need of help.

Today Al Collier is again a busy and determined businessman. His health has improved and relations with his stepson's dog are back to normal: Alex just ignores him.

— ASSESSMENT —

Q: Why do you think the two dogs stayed by the side of Al Collier when he was ill?

a) Perhaps Al was feeding them his meals. People who are ill don't eat much.

b) The dogs saw someone lying in bed all day and thought how comfortable it would be to join in.

c) The two dogs sensed that Al was ill and they were protecting him.

Q: Why would Alex the shih-tzu ignore Al once he became well again?

a) When Al is well, he is busy and can't be bothered with Alex either.

b) When Al is well, James is free to play with Alex.

c) When Alex senses a person's illness, he wants to help and comfort.

PET TEST No. 1: Is Your Pet a Comfort Bringer?

These simple questions will help you to decide if your pet has the power to comfort others. Simply tick the boxes next to the answers that best fit your pet. Then refer to the Pet Assessment Chart to discover whether your pet is a comforting helper.

1) When you're feeling sad, does your pet ever place its head on your knee or rub its body alongside your leg, looking up at you as if to say, "Don't cry, I'm your friend"?
a) ☐ It behaves this way when I'm not sad as well.
b) ☐ It looks up at me as if to say, "Where's my dinner?"
c) ☐ My pet knows when I am sad and cuddles up to me with love.

2) When you're ill in bed, maybe with an upset tummy or a bad cold, does your pet stand by your bedside as though on guard and protecting you?
a) ☐ My mother doesn't allow pets in the bedroom.
b) ☐ I'm sure my pet knows when I'm ill from the way it sits by my bed until I'm better.
c) ☐ My pet always wants to sleep on my bed, and if I'm ill it's there most of the time.

3) Do you talk to your pet, tell it your troubles? And does it seem to understand and comfort you?

a) ☐ I sometimes talk to my pet but it doesn't understand a word I say.

b) ☐ My pet listens to me and seems to respond with love.

c) ☐ I usually tell my troubles to a human. At least they don't run off to chase a fly just when I'm opening my heart.

4) Has your pet ever come running to your side to protect you in a moment of danger?

a) ☐ My moments of danger usually come in the school yard, when my pet is at home.

b) ☐ Maybe once; it may have been coincidence, though.

c) ☐ Definitely: I was in danger and suddenly my pet appeared by my side.

5) If someone in your house is ill, does your pet seem to know, and to alter its behavior?

a) ☐ Yes, my pet does know. It is much quieter if someone is sick.

b) ☐ It doesn't run about so much, but that may be because the rest of the family are being quiet.

c) ☐ My pet snoozes all day anyway.

6) Has your pet ever tried to warn you of a danger you were not aware of? Maybe an oncoming car that could have hit you, or a fire you hadn't seen?

a) ☐ Perhaps it did once, I just can't be certain.

b) ☐ My pet did once warn me of a danger I hadn't noticed.

c) ☐ I'm the one who has to keep my pet from getting run over, not the other way round.

7) If you have injured some part of your body, does your pet seem to be aware of this? Maybe it presses up to your injured limb as though to warm it with its body?

a) ☐ It may do. I have noticed my pet seems aware of my state of health.

b) ☐ It's more likely to trip me up and run away.

c) □ My pet knows if I've hurt myself and gently presses itself up against where I am injured. I'm sure it's trying to heal me.

8) Has your pet ever tried to help an injured or sick animal? For example, by nuzzling it gently or licking its wound?
a) □ My pet never bothers with other animals at all.
b) □ Yes, my pet does nuzzle up to injured or sick animals.
c) □ My pet may try to go to sick or injured animals, but I don't let it.

Total your score

Each question had three choices: a, b, or c. Each choice has a score: 0, 1, or 2. Check your answers, total your score, and refer to the Pet Assessment Chart.

Q1: a) 1 b) 0 c) 2 **Q2:** a) 0 b) 2 c) 1 **Q3:** a) 1 b) 2 c) 0
Q4: a) 0 b) 1 c) 2 **Q5:** a) 2 b) 1 c) 0 **Q6:** a) 1 b) 2 c) 0
Q7: a) 1 b) 0 c) 2 **Q8:** a) 0 b) 2 c) 1

— Pet Assessment Chart —

16–10: You have a caring and very loving pet. Treasure this friend. **9–5:** Your pet is trying to help others. Encourage it with your love. **4–0:** You are the proud owner of a pet lawnmower. Keep it oiled.

SIMO: The Healing Dolphin

Imagine living your life alone in a dark room, unable to love or be loved. Depression is like that.

Bill Bowell was suffering badly. The doctors had tried everything to cure him – tablets, injections, hospital, hypnosis. Bill's family loved him dearly. His five children were desperate to bring back the man they were proud to call Dad. His wife Edna refused to give in. Every day she and the children made some attempt to reach into her husband's darkness. But no matter what they tried, Bill remained a prisoner of clinical depression.

Wales and dolphins

In the summer of 1986, Edna decided to take the family away on holiday. For almost twelve years Bill had been a sick man, struggling against the mental pain that crippled him as surely as if he had been bound. Perhaps some sea air might release him.

Edna drove the family up from Oxford to Wales, to the Pembrokeshire coastal village of Solva, near St. David's. They had hired an old stone cottage for a week. The fresh air would do all of them good and there is always plenty of that on the Pembrokeshire coast.

On the first night of the holiday Mrs. Bowell suggested they all go into the village and visit the local pub, the Harbour Hotel. Bill didn't mind. He never minded anything: nothing mattered to him, nothing at all.

Inside the hotel, Susan, the eldest daughter, ordered the drinks while Edna settled Bill in a corner seat. Looking around, she saw a notice board and went up to it. There was a handwritten notice announcing a meeting that night at a nearby hall. A talk and film show would be given by a Dr. Dobbs. The subject was dolphins.

Edna thought it might be an idea to go along to the lecture. When she asked Bill if he wanted to go, he replied, "Yes please." By ordinary standards this is not a tremendous response, but Bill hardly ever spoke and was not usually keen enough even to say please.

A date with a dolphin

The film showed dolphins swimming freely in the sea. Afterward Dr. Dobbs gave a short talk. He said he was in Solva to make another film and conduct research.

When Dr. Dobbs talked about dolphins, it was as if he

were speaking directly to Bill. He seemed to be offering a chance for Bill to climb out of his darkness into the light. The pictures of those dolphins swimming had created a weird feeling deep inside him.

After the talk had ended, Bill did something he hadn't done in years: he went up and spoke to a stranger. Dr. Dobbs listened politely, but told Bill that he was a very busy man. But Bill's daughter Karen was not going to leave it there. She followed Dr. Dobbs to the door and asked him to help her father. She told him how desperate the family were to bring back to life the man they all loved. Dr. Dobbs must have been impressed by her determination, because he agreed to take Bill out to see the dolphins. He told Karen that if she and the family could get Bill Bowell onto the harbor wall at ten o'clock the next morning, he could join that day's crew on the boat going out into St. Bride's Bay to meet a dolphin called Simo.

Bill swims in the sea

The following day, at exactly 10 A.M., Dr. Dobbs welcomed Bill on board his boat. He had brought with him a flask of hot coffee and some sandwiches prepared by Karen and Susan. They were determined that their dad was not going to miss this chance at experiencing something new. They hoped it might give Bill back the will to live that he had lost so many years ago.

About half an hour out into St. Bride's Bay, round Ramsey Island and past St. David's Head, the skipper pointed the boat into a secluded bay. As the boat coasted about fifty yards out from the rugged shoreline, Bill saw a fin cutting through the green water. "That's Simo," said Dr. Dobbs.

Bill's heart beat faster as he watched the dolphin approach the boat. Closer and closer it came; he could see the outline of the animal now, steel grey in the pale sea lit by the morning sunlight, streaking gracefully through the waves.

Suddenly Simo the dolphin burst through the foam and, swishing his powerful tail, stood straight up alongside the boat right next to Bill Bowell. From the moment Bill looked into Simo's eyes, he was transfixed. Without thinking, he reached forward and touched the dolphin's head. A thought jumped into his mind: "We need each other." How long he was leaning forward and stroking the dolphin, Bill doesn't know. Time stood still. All that mattered was the thought that the dolphin loved and needed him.

Dr. Dobbs, watching very carefully, had seen the joy spreading through Bill Bowell as, for the first time in twelve years, the man smiled. "He says we need each other," Bill said. "Simo needs me." There were tears of pure happiness running down his face. In that brief encounter with the dolphin, Bill had begun to unlock the door of his personal prison cell. Simo had given him the key, a key called love.

Quickly Dr. Dobbs dressed Bill Bowell in a diver's wet-suit. It didn't fit very well, because Bill had taken no exercise at all during his long illness, but they got it on him. Then Dr. Dobbs helped Bill slip over the side of the boat to swim with Simo the dolphin.

It was the first time he had been in the sea for years. Perhaps Simo sensed this, for within seconds he was swimming alongside Bill and gently pushing him up, keeping him afloat with his nose.

As Bill Bowell swam with Simo, he began to feel that the

dolphin was trying to tell him something very important. When he looked into Simo's eyes, the message registered in his mind. The dolphin was saying, "I need you! Please come and share my mysterious world." The shock made Bill almost cry out loud. He became lost in that beautiful creature's magical company, swam like an athlete and forgot completely that he was a sick man.

Bill is transformed

"Mr. Bowell! Come in, Mr. Bowell!"

Bill was surprised to hear himself summoned back. It only seemed like a few minutes that he had been with Simo, and the dolphin needed him. But in fact Bill had been swimming with Simo for almost an hour. It took quite a bit of persuading to get him back on board, because he was so enthralled by the dolphin.

Dr. Dobbs was delighted with Bill's response to swimming with Simo and invited him along on the following and final day of his dolphin observations. Once again, Bill was transformed by that magnificent creature. So changed was he that Dr. Dobbs asked the boat owner if he would consider taking Bill out himself after Dr. Dobbs and the camera team had left. The man at once agreed; he could see how much the dolphin meant to Bill.

Each morning for the rest of the week's holiday, the boatman met Bill Bowell at the harbor wall and took him out to swim with Simo the dolphin. Bill believes that Simo saved his life, because by the end of the seven days he had almost shaken off his long illness.

Simo makes medical history

In the months after Bill's meeting with Dr. Dobbs, they kept in contact. The doctor wanted to assess the long-term effect that swimming with the dolphin might have. Bill's wife and all his children often answered Dr. Dobbs's calls with the marvellous news that Bill was, almost miraculously, healed. Not that this surprised the good doctor. He had always thought that dolphins could have a positive effect on human beings suffering from clinical depression. Now he had the living proof: Bill Bowell was cured.

Since that first meeting with Simo, Bill has swum with other dolphins. Dr. Dobbs took him to Ireland to meet a very beautiful dolphin called Funghie, who immediately befriended Bill. Together they swam in the seas around the Irish coast, rubbing noses, diving, dancing in the cool green waves, and, Bill felt, sharing the joy of just being alive together.

Bill says that there is an energy force that seems to enter his body as he swims with dolphins. This force invigorates him, fills him with a delight in living that had been locked away all those long, dark years when he was ill. Now Bill only has to see a dolphin to feel better. But he just can't stand to watch captive dolphins, not after swimming with them in the wild. Even the old films of Flipper are instantly switched off in the Bowell household.

Today Bill Bowell is living testimony to the healing powers of dolphins. Specialist physicians from all over the world have attended, by invitation of Dr. Dobbs, to watch Bill Bowell and the dolphins together. The pioneering work of Dr. Dobbs and the example of Mr. Bowell did much to bring about the international appreciation of the healing powers of dolphins. Since then, many unhappy people have enjoyed dolphin cures.

— ASSESSMENT —

Q1. Do you think Simo the dolphin really spoke telepathically to Bill?

a) Dolphins don't know English. And why would it need Bill?

b) Bill probably believed the dolphin communicated its thoughts to him because he was ill at the time.

c) Simo projected his thoughts into Bill's mind by telepathy. Bill received these thoughts as images and translated them into words that he understood.

Q2. Was Bill actually cured by Simo and Funghie, the two dolphins?

a) Perhaps the shock of the cold sea water snapped him out of his depression.

b) The strange experience of being in the sea with a dolphin made Bill realize that life can be fun. Therefore he cured himself.

c) The dolphins gave Bill all the love and affection they had to give and, in some mysterious way, took over his mind, wiping away the dark clouds of depression.

MOUSE: The Cat Who Cared

Paul G. Stout had been a member of the U.S. Coast Guard for twenty-one years. He was a strong and active man, and his extensive duties, which included search and rescue missions at sea, made this a really exciting job. Then, after what seemed like a lifetime's service, he retired.

A lonely life

It was a shock at first. Paul missed the teamwork and the special sense of belonging that goes with it. But he was determined his working life would continue. So, after taking a further degree course in Phoenix, Arizona, he moved to the town of Kent about 20 miles south of Seattle in the state of Washington, where he had been promised a job. Living alone, he tried to make friends, but the locals seemed to have their lives to live and he was a stranger. It

33

was a very lonely time for Paul and, when the job failed to materialize, he became deeply depressed.

Each morning Paul would rise early and walk through the fields and woods that surround the little town of Kent. There he could at least experience the beauty of nature and see the trees blowing in the soft wind coming in from the Pacific Ocean with salt on its breath. Back home, if his solitary apartment could be called that, he read the newspapers and applied for job after job. With growing anxiety, Paul realized that he had no one to turn to for help. Unlike most of the other folks in Kent, he was a man on his own and he worried that he would always be alone.

Unexpected guests

It was during the September of his first year in the new area that Paul discovered a litter of feral kittens. He had often seen the mother cat running wild in the streets near his apartment and had once fed her some fish bits left over from a meal. When the cat was about to give birth, she had found shelter under the wooden veranda outside Paul's apartment.

Quite what made him look there, Paul doesn't know. Perhaps it was the faint cry of the little kittens as they called out in hunger for a mother who could never return to feed them. For when Paul looked under the boards he could see the dead body of the wild cat, who had survived only a few days after giving birth. Gently he placed her lifeless body in an old box to bury later that day.

But now he had to do something for the living. He reached down and lifted the tiny kittens out from under the wooden boards. There were four of them, and all were desperately weak. Carrying them carefully in his hands, he took them into his apartment and placed them softly on an old towel. Their little eyes had barely opened and each tiny mouth was reaching for food. Rushing to the fridge, Paul found some milk and poured it into a saucer, but the kittens were too young to feed this way. Then he had an idea. In the bathroom he found an eyedropper. He filled it with milk and dripped the liquid into the kittens' mouths.

For hours and hours Paul cared for the kittens. They were brown and black, mainly, and very cute, but so tiny and weak. They seemed endlessly hungry and soon he was completely out of milk. Grabbing his overcoat, Paul ran out into the dark September night to buy some more from a nearby all-night store.

He couldn't have been gone more than half an hour, but when he returned, three of the little kittens were quiet and still. They were resting, Paul thought. But when he reached to touch them, their tiny bodies were already growing cold. In the short time it had taken him to fetch the milk, they had died. One by one he took each of the kittens outside and placed it in the old cardboard box next to their dead mother. For them life's struggle was over.

The survivor

Back inside his apartment, Paul filled the glass eyedropper again and gently fed the surviving kitten. Right through the darkest hours he nursed it. The night turned into a pale dawn and still the kitten lived. "Come on, pal," said Paul to the little brown bundle of fur, no bigger than the palm of his hand. "You can make it if you try!"

There was something about this small creature that reminded him of someone. It had not a friend in the whole world, not even a mother to feed it or a sister to cuddle up to. This kitten was all alone. Then Paul realized – the kitten was just like him.

For a second his heart beat faster. They had each other now. Paul had the friend he had longed for all those months as a stranger in a strange town. Now, just as his life was slipping into hopeless despair, he had found another he could share each day with. No longer would he be alone. "Please God, let it live," he said and held the kitten close to his chest, as a mother might hold a newborn baby.

Over the next few weeks the kitten grew stronger. Paul fed it first from the eyedropper, then from his hand. To that kitten he was its mother and he cared for it with all his heart. The kitten was female and Paul called her Mouse, because she was little bigger than one and quite as cheeky. The little cat would jump up and sit on Paul's knee whenever she got the chance. Everywhere he went, there was Mouse, poking her funny face into the morning newspaper, into the cornflakes, into the sink; she was a proper nosy little cat.

Mouse makes the difference

Weeks turned to months and Paul had never been as happy. Mouse was his friend and each day seemed like fun with her around up to tricks. The cat followed Paul all over the place, getting stronger and stronger all the time. Until one day, just before Christmas, Mouse followed Paul out of the apartment on his early morning walk into the woods outside the town.

And from then on, each morning saw big Paul marching through the streets whistling a tune with a tiny tabby cat trotting along at his side. It might have looked odd, but it made Paul feel so proud. He had saved this cat, yet in a way the cat had saved him. Since he had taken little Mouse into his life, Paul had changed. No longer did he view each day with dread. Now he really had something to live for; now he had a friend that cared for him.

The new positive Paul quickly found a job. Perhaps there was something more likeable, more relaxed about him with Mouse as his pet. Somehow the love of that little cat had welcomed Paul into the community, made him feel truly at home.

Over the next eight years Paul shared every day with Mouse, the tiny pussycat. Everywhere he went she followed. Each morning, just as dawn broke, the two friends could be seen walking through the woods together, enjoying the fresh northwest wind blowing in from the sea. The salt breeze brought back happy memories to Paul's mind, of the days when his team consisted of more than a little cat.

Addition and loss

Paul even bought another cat to keep Mouse company while he was at work. He called this one Briefcase, because one day the new kitten had trapped itself inside his case and caused quite a sensation when Paul had opened it at work. The two cats and Paul got on really well together, playing all sorts of crazy games.

Then, while still a young cat, Mouse became seriously ill. Paul did everything possible for his friend, took her to the vet and paid for the very best treatment, but nothing could be done. It was with a heavy heart that he made the final decision for his little Mouse. In all his years as a Coast Guardsman no decision had been harder to make.

That night Paul sat quietly in his apartment holding Briefcase on his knee, thinking of his friend. He remembered the day he had found the litter of kittens and how he had nursed the tiny Mouse. And he thought of all the joy her friendship had brought. Finding the kitten had helped him to find himself. To others Mouse might have seemed just a funny little cat, but to Paul she would always be the friend that came when his need was greatest. He knew he would never forget the cat that cared when no one else in the whole world did.

— ASSESSMENT —

Q1. Was Mouse the best thing that could have happened to Paul?

a) He needed a job and some friends; he would have done better to join a club or do voluntary work.

b) Paul needed someone to love and care for, and the kitten fitted the bill.

c) That kitten was meant for Paul. They were alike and their friendship was special.

Q2. In what way do you think Mouse helped Paul?

a) Paul was fed up being on his own, and having a cat made him feel less lonely.

b) Before Paul found Mouse he had no friends in town; when he found the cat, all that changed. The love he received from his pet gave him confidence.

c) By saving the life of little Mouse, Paul proved to himself that his life had purpose. With Mouse by his side, Paul was once again needed and loved by another living creature.

ZILLAH: Joanne's Guide Dog

Joanne Paterson was born with seriously impaired vision. As a child she could see a little and was managing fairly well, receiving lots of help and encouragement from her very caring parents, Jean and Keith Paterson. They even moved home so that Joanne could attend a special school for the partially sighted at Preston, in Lancashire, England.

Unfortunately Joanne's sight gradually deteriorated. By the time she was sixteen years old, this pretty girl was totally blind. Never again would she see the smiling faces of her mother and father, who had tried so hard to enable her to cope. Now Joanne would have to live in endless darkness.

Ignorance is blindness

Life must go on, and Joanne was as determined as any other young person to be independent. Like all teenagers, she wanted to enjoy herself among people of her own age group. She persuaded her parents to let her go to a residential college for the blind in Hereford, England.

Two years later, Joanne returned home to Preston. It was a difficult time for her and her parents, who wanted their daughter to live life to the full. This was almost impossible as her walks out of the house were limited to very familiar streets. Joanne had only a long white cane to feel her way forward and was frequently in danger not only from passing traffic but also from some thoughtless members of the public. As strange as it may seem, there are some sighted people who are even blinder than Joanne. Often she would be bumped and jostled as she tried, as best she could, to make her way to the local shops. Joanne at first thought these people hadn't recognized her disability, but in time she realized they just didn't care. Joanne was really worried that one day she might be seriously injured by some careless person. Keith tried to comfort her by saying that ignorance is the very worst form of blindness in the world.

Joanne had already applied for a guide dog, or seeing-eye dog. At her school they had told her how these wonderful creatures helped many blind people to enjoy a fuller life. She could hardly wait.

Training for dogs and people

The Guide Dogs for the Blind school in Bolton, Lancashire, runs courses for prospective owners. The courses are residential and last for three weeks. This enables the dog and the owner to learn how to work together as a team. The dogs, usually labradors or golden retrievers, are already trained. This takes many months. From puppies they are walked and taught street drill, traffic sense, personal control, and how to react in the special harness that they wear, which gives the blind person a much better feel for the dog than an ordinary lead. With time and practice, dog and owner become a team with a real understanding of each other's actions.

When Joanne was nineteen, she received the long-awaited telephone call from Guide Dogs for the Blind, telling her to attend in November for training with the dog they had for her.

At the school all those attending the course were introduced to their tutor and had the details of the next three weeks briefly explained to them. Then each was taken to their private room, to meet their guide dog for the first time. Joanne was very nervous. What if the dog didn't like her? Hearing the door open, she sat up straight and held out her hand. Into it was pressed the softest, wettest nose she had ever felt.

"This is Zillah," the tutor said. Joanne reached out and stroked the Labrador. She whispered her name and some words of welcome. She really hoped they would be pals. The dog seemed quite friendly and rubbed its body against

Joanne's legs. As she sat there gently ruffling the big dog's fur, a sense of hope spread through her. With the help of Zillah she would be free to venture out into the world that had been denied her for so long.

Over the next three weeks, Zillah and Joanne learned how to work together. The tutor took both of them out into the streets of Bolton, which is a busy town. There they practised crossing roads, walking down crowded streets, and even climbing stairs. It was an exciting time for Joanne. And all the while she was looking forward to going home to try out her new passport to freedom, Zillah the guide dog, all on her own.

The reluctant guide dog

Back in Preston, after the residential course, Joanne was joined by her tutor at her parents' home. Now she was taught how to work with Zillah in her own area. The tutor followed Joanne and the guide dog through the neighboring streets, getting the dog used to this new and unfamiliar place. Then, just before Christmas, Joanne was ready to take Zillah out on her own. Fastening Zillah into her harness, she put on her coat and set off on a new adventure.

As they turned the third corner leading down to the newsagents on the main road, Zillah stopped. She sat down and wouldn't move. "Come on, Zillah," Joanne said, trying to get her guide dog to walk, but the Labrador just wouldn't. For a few minutes Joanne wondered what to do. She knew where she was and how to get home, but Zillah wasn't for joining her. The dog had simply stopped. There was no danger Joanne could sense – she could hear no traffic, sense no pushing crowds, just the empty, windswept streets.

Time passed but Zillah refused to move. Joanne was standing there, cold, confused and miserable. She couldn't just leave the dog. What should she do? Panic set in. All these months she had dreamed about being out and free with her own guide dog and now – now she was stuck! For one awful minute she almost gave in to the tears starting in her eyes as despair swept through her body. All her hopes seemed to have failed. Why me? she thought. Why my dog?

Eventually Zillah stood up and Joanne turned for home. For days she said nothing to her parents, not wanting them to see how sad she was. But she told her tutor, who visited regularly. The problem turned out to be that Zillah had grown deeply attached to the Guide Dogs for the Blind tutor and thought she was her owner. She hadn't yet fully accepted that she was now Joanne's dog. That would take a little time.

A dog's Christmas

Joanne had an idea. She got her father to move the dog's box to the foot of her bed, and each night and morning she personally let Zillah in and out of the house. Joanne also undertook all the dog's care, feeding her and combing her fur, which she knew was golden, though she could not see it. Soon it would be Christmas and she would buy Zillah some presents to welcome her properly into the Paterson family.

On Christmas morning Joanne got up early to give Zillah the squeaky toys and rubber bones she had bought for her. It had only just turned six o'clock when she woke the dog. Zillah enjoyed the toys and seemed to know that they were a special treat from her owner. All that care and attention had helped to create a bond between them, and Joanne felt confident that Zillah understood that she was her dog now. That afternoon she decided to try again on her own with the guide dog.

At the third corner from her home, Zillah again stopped. A feeling of dread filled Joanne's mind. "Come on, Zillah," she said, trying to encourage the dog to walk on, but it wouldn't move.

Suddenly a car zoomed past, travelling at high speed. This time, Zillah was only doing her job.

It was a glorious feeling for Joanne, being out with Zillah all on her own. She loved her parents and her home, but to be free, to be out in the world and independent, that was what she wanted. Zillah would give her that freedom. It was the very best Christmas present that Joanne had ever received.

A future for Joanne

Over the years that Zillah and Joanne have been together, they have developed a real bond of understanding and love. Through the selfless help of her guide dog, Joanne has grown more and more confident. One thing that she has noticed is how much more understanding people seem to be when they see her walking with her guide dog. Joanne's previous experiences of others' blind ignorance are rarely repeated when she has Zillah by her side. Now she frequently walks out in the busy streets of Preston to meet her new boyfriend Rob. Together they are talking positively about their lives. Joanne is looking forward to a future that seemed but a dream those few years ago, when she was trapped in the country of the blind, before she met Zillah.

— ASSESSMENT —

Q1. What do you think was the main factor in forming a bond between Joanne and the guide dog?
a) The long absences of the tutor whom the dog had previously bonded with.
b) The extra attention and the toys.
c) Joanne's affectionate care for the dog even when it wasn't helping her as she had hoped.

Q2. Why do you think people are more understanding when they see Joanne with Zillah?
a) Some people are frightened that the dog might bite them if they push Joanne.
b) The guide dog is a clear and recognized sign that Joanne is blind. It is also more visible than a white cane.
c) The influence of a dog makes people gentle.

VINNIE: The Cat That Cured a Migraine

Jeanne Garner, who lives in the town of Lexington, Oklahoma, USA, was a very sick person when she first welcomed Vinnie the cat into her home. Her life was spoiled by headaches, not just little ones that hurt a bit behind the forehead and disappear with a couple of tablets, but really serious ones. Doctors at her local hospital told her she was suffering from migraine attacks.

Often Jeanne would be so ill with these awful headaches that she would have to go into a dark room and lie down. The pain was unbearable and, when it was at it worst, the vision in her eyes would become really distorted.

Then one day, at a vet's office, she saw a bedraggled stray

cat that was due to be put to sleep. It had been abandoned, no one wanted this cat. Jeanne took one look and asked if she could have him. The vet agreed.

Jeanne called the cat Vinnie and took him home. He quickly became Jeanne's best pal. He would snuggle up on her knee as she watched TV, and followed her everywhere she went. Then one busy afternoon, while Jeanne was working on her computer, she was struck by the most horrible headache she had ever suffered.

Healing paws

Jeanne knew exactly what she had to do: go into her bedroom, draw the heavy velvet curtains, switch off the lights, and lie down. The terrible buzzing feeling pounded through her brain and her eyes began to blur as the migraine attack took control. She was helpless, locked into a world of pure pain.

Then, as she lay in the darkness, she felt something gently stroking her neck and shoulders. Jeanne relaxed as the soothing pressure smoothed away the awful pain. For a moment she did not think about who was massaging her, she just enjoyed the release it brought.

Slowly the migraine attack passed. When Jeanne switched on the bedside lamp, she saw Vinnie the cat sitting on the pillow by the side of her head. It had been her pet cat that had been softly stroking away the hurt from her head. Vinnie had somehow known that his best pal was in pain. With his little paws on Jeanne's neck, he had eased the terrible tension from her taut muscles.

Two amazing recoveries

For years afterward, Vinnie helped Jeanne in this way. Each time she had a migraine attack, he would follow her into the darkened bedroom and stroke away the blinding pain she was suffering.

Gradually, and neither Jeanne nor her doctors can explain how, her migraine attacks disappeared. It wasn't an overnight cure, but slowly they became less frequent. Months began to pass between the headache attacks, and one day she realized she was cured. Jeanne believes that cure has something to do with the loving attention of her cat Vinnie. She thinks that the cat was sent to help in her hour of need, like a special gift bestowed from the mysterious world beyond.

Twelve years after Vinnie first entered Jeanne's life, it was Jeanne's turn to help the cat, for he was diagnosed as having a kidney complaint. The vet did not think he could live, but Jeanne refused to accept this and decided to try a different form of treatment. Using the Japanese *reiki* method of channelling the energy or life force fundamental to traditional Oriental medicine, Jeanne has helped Vinnie to live. Just as Vinnie helped her all those years before.

Vinnie's recovery astounded the vets. Jeanne believes that the power of healing she shares with the cat begins within their loving hearts. As each cares for the other, so the power increases. To her, Vinnie is one very special cat.

— ASSESSMENT —

Q: Why do you think Vinnie stroked Jeanne's head?

a) The cat followed her everywhere. When she lay down, he curled up by her head. She perceived his movements as deliberate stroking.

b) Vinnie was trying to comfort Jeanne and put his paws on her as if she were a sick kitten.

c) Vinnie has special healing powers in his paws and used these to stroke away Jeanne's migraine.

Q: What do you think cured Jeanne's migraine headaches?

a) Any of a number of factors we have not been told about, such as a change in her diet.

b) The love she felt for Vinnie helped Jeanne relax and eased the stress that may have caused the headaches.

c) Vinnie's concentrated healing power of love cured Jeanne. The cat has mysterious powers.

PET TEST No. 2:
Can Your Pet Cure a Headache?

By conducting this simple test, you can discover whether your pet can help someone to get rid of a headache. Just follow these straightforward steps and then complete the assessment at the end.

1) Seek a volunteer from your close friends or family, someone who often gets headaches.

2) Explain the experiment to the volunteer by saying something like this:

"I'm trying to test my pet to see if it can cure headaches. If you agree to participate, all you need do is tell me when you are suffering from a headache and then let me bring my pet to you." (If your pet is a boa constrictor, volunteers may be hard to find.)

3) Introduce your volunteer to your pet so that they know what to expect when the time comes.

4) Tell your pet what is expected. Try talking to it gently and always think positive thoughts as you do so.

5) When you receive the call from your volunteer, tell him or her to:
a) sit or lie down on a comfortable chair or settee;
b) relax by taking long, slow breaths;
c) prepare to meet your pet.

6) Take your pet to the volunteer and watch carefully the way it behaves around the sick person. Note its actions on the assessment form (below).

7) After fifteen to thirty minutes, ask your volunteer to answer the questions on the assessment form and note the answers.

— Assessment Form —

Pet Observations

Observe pet during the period from introduction to volunteer to end of experiment. Look at the lists below and place a tick in the boxes that most closely match the actions of your pet.

Pet's Reaction to Suffering Headache Volunteer

	YES	NO	MAYBE
1) Pet tried to comfort volunteer.	☐	☐	☐
2) Pet fell asleep.	☐	☐	☐
3) Pet snuggled up to the volunteer.	☐	☐	☐
4) Pet licked volunteer's head.	☐	☐	☐
5) Pet chewed volunteer's nose.	☐	☐	☐
6) Pet made friendly noises to volunteer.	☐	☐	☐
7) Pet gently pawed or stroked volunteer.	☐	☐	☐
8) Pet ruffled hair of volunteer, as if searching for nits.	☐	☐	☐
9) Pet shoved its nose into volunteer's face.	☐	☐	☐
10) Pet shoved claws or paws into volunteer's mouth.	☐	☐	☐

Volunteer's Reaction to Pet

Ask your volunteer to select the two answers most closely matching their experience.

1) This was a very relaxing experience with a nice pet. ☐

2) My headache went during this test and I believe the pet cured me. ☐

3) Pass the Band-Aids! My lawyer has your name and address. ☐

4) Nothing much happened but I enjoyed the test. ☐

5) I thought the pet was a positive influence and it did seem to help. ☐

6) Can't be sure if the pet did it, but my headache has gone. ☐

7) My headache is now much worse – a total failure. ☐

8) My headache is slightly better so perhaps your pet did help. ☐

9) My clothes are ruined. What are you feeding that thing on? ☐

10) The pet was very comforting and it made me feel better. ☐

— Pet's Assessment —

Q.1 Yes: 3 No: 0 Maybe: 1   **Q.2** Yes: 0 No: 3 Maybe: 1
Q.3 Yes: 3 No: 0 Maybe: 1   **Q.4** Yes: 3 No: 0 Maybe: 1
Q.5 Yes: 0 No: 3 Maybe: 1   **Q.6** Yes: 3 No: 0 Maybe: 1
Q.7 Yes: 3 No: 0 Maybe: 1   **Q.8** Yes: 1 No: 0 Maybe: 3
Q.9 Yes: 3 No: 0 Maybe: 1   **Q.10** Yes: 1 No: 0 Maybe: 3

ADD TOTAL SCORE:_____

— Volunteer's Assessment —

Q.1 Yes: 5   **Q.2** Yes: 10
Q.3 Yes: minus 10   **Q.4** Yes: 3
Q.5 Yes: 5   **Q.6** Yes: 5
Q.7 Yes: minus 5   **Q.8** Yes: 7
Q.9 Yes: minus 10   **Q.10** Yes: 10

ADD TOTAL SCORE:_____

Now add together both the above totals and refer to the final assessment below:

FINAL TOTAL IS:_____

50–35 points: You have a pet that can cure headaches and comfort people.

34–19 points: Your pet has the ability to develop its comforting skills but you must encourage it.

18–0 points: Exactly what sort of pet have you, a vampire bat?

PIGLET AND THE GIRLS: At the Camomile Centre

Piglet

Throughout the world there are places where people with disabilities can go to enjoy the therapeutic experience of being with animals. Within Dartmoor National Park in the county of Devon, England, high on a hill overlooking the mysterious moorland is just such a place. At the end of steep, winding lane, where the woodlands part into a cobbled farmyard, is the Camomile Centre, founded by Helen Cottington. It is the most wonderful place. There are horses to ride, donkeys, a lovely pony, hens, rabbits, dogs, and even a little vegetable garden.

One of the resident therapy horses at the Camomile Centre is called Piglet. He is quite a big horse, very strong and fifteen hands in height. This chestnut cob has a beautiful flaxen mane and tail which he swishes from side to side whenever he greets his special friends. One of Piglet's friends is an eighteen-year-old called Richard Holman. Richard lives in a little town near Bovey Tracey, just a few miles from the center. He visits the center at least once a week to ride.

I saw them together on a rainy day early in August 1997. Dartmoor was shrouded in the kind of mist that makes one think of the Hound of the Baskervilles and haunted castles. At three o'clock Richard arrived, holding his hard hat. He was looking forward to riding his favourite horse, Piglet. Richard's father Peter watched with a degree of pride as his son tried to place his riding hat on his head. The center staff supervised Richard and prepared him for his equestrian adventure. Outside in the yard Piglet was patiently waiting.

Then Piglet trotted ahead to the paddock from the yard and Richard followed, with the staff close at hand. Watching the young man making his way to ride Piglet, I was aware that this was what he wanted to do. I could sense the determination in each of his faltering, often hesitant steps. He walked with great difficulty, being severely physically disabled, but he walked. There was fun at the end of this little journey and Richard was going to get there.

Inside the wood-fenced arena, assisted by the staff, Richard climbed up on the mounting platform and was helped into the horse's saddle. Being totally deaf and almost completely blind, he lives under close supervision. Whenever his parents are not by his side, there are trained staff and carers to watch over him. Except when he is riding Piglet. On top of that horse Richard is alone, as independent as he will ever be.

As soon as Piglet felt Richard's hand on him, the horse turned and swished his flaxen mane, brushing it softly against his fingers. The horse's tail swung up and flicked from side to side as if welcoming his friend. All these little signals seemed to register on Richard's face as his senses tuned in to the happy experience of being on horseback. With his hands gripping the saddle and his feet firmly in the stirrups, Richard was ready to ride.

As if someone in the heavens had been watching for this moment, the rain stopped. The clouds parted and sunshine shone down on the woods and green, rolling hills. In the far distance, as the sun lifted the drifting mist, we could see the Dartmoor marsh grass leading out to Cornwall and the faraway sea.

The staff took Piglet's reins and led him out of the paddock into the lane. At each turn of the path the horse halted and checked his rider. At one junction he stopped dead still, his ears pricking up. No one moved. Then a car turned the corner into the path where we would have been but for Piglet. He had obviously heard the oncoming vehicle and had acted to protect his friend in the saddle.

I could see the concentration on Richard's face. He was balanced perfectly on that horse. For mile after mile he rode, up hill and down the thorn-hedged paths across the moors, circling the Camomile Centre. Piglet appeared to understand exactly what was required of him with regard to giving his friend Richard a safe ride. The special care was evident in each step the horse took.

In the paddock Richard's father was waiting, together with Helen Cottington. When Richard returned, they watched as the staff helped him off Piglet. Then he walked slowly back and gripped the safety of his father's arm. On Richard's face there was just the hint of a secret smile. He had enjoyed that ride. "You did well, son," said Peter. Although Richard could not hear, I knew that he understood. I think Piglet did too, for as we walked together into the farmyard stables, the big horse shook its glorious mane and whinnied in that funny way horses only do when they are absolutely happy.

The girls

Can you imagine having hens as your friends? Looking after farmyard poultry might not be everyone's idea of fun, but to one client of the Camomile Centre hens mean a great deal. David Mullen, a former soldier, used to live and work in his home town of Newton Abbot, Devon. One day when David was forty-five, as he was crossing the main road, he was knocked down and almost killed by a speeding car.

For months David's life hung in the balance. He was in a coma and even the best surgeons in England thought he would die. Time passed and still David failed to open his eyes. The months turned to a year and all hope seemed lost. Then, after one and a half years in a total coma, David awoke. But he could neither walk nor talk.

After months and months of therapy in hospital, David was finally allowed to go home. His speech had returned, but he was confined to a wheelchair, dependent on others' help, and he had lost all memory of most of his past. His army days and working life were as if they had never been. He could remember only very recent events and the distant days of his childhood.

I met David at the Camomile Centre, where he goes at least twice a week. His broad shoulders and firm jaw impressed me, but the wheelchair and those trembling hands told a different story. He told me that his grandmother had taught him to love and respect all God's creatures. As a boy on a farm outside Newton Abbot, he had got to know pigs, turkeys, geese, and hens. David liked the hens best of all. His grandmother used to let him feed them, and they would come and peck the food out of his hands. These were the kind of things David remembered.

As we talked, I could sense that something of great importance to this gentle man was about to be revealed to me. "Do you want to meet the girls?" he said with a twinkle in his eye, as though he were back on that far distant farm. "Grandmother says I've got to look after God's creatures."

It was no easy task for David to lead me to the hens. His electric wheelchair whirred and struggled up the incline leading to the immaculately clean wooden hut. Opening the door required great effort and concentration on David's part. But he would not give in. Up he rode to the door and grabbed the string that enabled him to release the catch. Then we were in.

There were hens here, there, and everywhere, hopping and cackling. Scooping up a handful of grain from a metal feeding tray, David held out his hand, and a Rhode Island Red farmyard hen came and pecked away at it. "These are my girls," he said.

For a few minutes I stood and watched as hen after hen came up to David. There were black and white plump ones, taller skinny all black ones, noisy ones, and a little shy young one that hid in the corner before it gathered up courage to join the others. They clucked and fluttered their feathers, pecking happily at the grain he had scattered. David sat in his wheelchair smiling with delight.

Back outside the hut, David showed me how he cleaned out the nests where the hens laid eggs. "I make marmalade sponge cakes from their eggs," he said. "It's good too."

Soon it was time for me to leave the Camomile Centre. The early August evening was turning to dusk and the sun was falling fast behind the lonely Dartmoor hills. As I turned to wave goodbye to Helen Cottington and her staff, I saw that David had wheeled himself out into the old cobbled yard. Before leaving, I shook his hand. "Tell them about my girls," he said, with a gentle, half-aware smile in his eyes. And I have.

— ASSESSMENT —

Q1. Do you believe that Piglet takes extra care of Richard because of his disability?
a) Not really. The horse is well trained and just follows a set routine.
b) It could be that Piglet is a very sensitive horse and is always careful with his riders.
c) Piglet probably senses that Richard has special needs as he cannot give the horse any of the usual signals. Being aware of this, Piglet takes extra care.

Q2. Why do you think David is happy with the hens?
a) He is no longer able to be with other people as an equal.
b) They remind him of his happy childhood on a farm.
c) The hens give David a sense of purpose in his life. By caring for them and receiving their friendship in return he feels happy and contented.

TABBY CAT:
The Life Saver

Carol Fowler lives in Billinge on the outskirts of Wigan, Lancashire, England. She shares a neat little flat with her husband Bob and her pet, Tabby Cat. One day in October 1996, Carol cut her finger on a rusty nail while tidying her back garden. Bob was out at work and Carol was alone with Tabby Cat.

The wound was not serious but, to be on the safe side, Carol decided to go to the doctor for an anti-tetanus jab. The doctor cleaned and dressed the cut and gave Carol the injection, to prevent the disease from infecting her. On the way home from the surgery Carol began to feel very faint. Her vision became blurred and it was only with great effort that she made it back to her home. As she pushed open the front door, all her strength failed and she fell down on the floor, unconscious. Carol had suffered an allergic reaction to the injection and her body was in shock.

Tabby Cat saw his friend on the floor and was alarmed. Clawing open the half-closed door, the cat ran out of the flat, crossed the hallway to the next-door neighbors, and began jumping up and hitting the metal letter-box flap on their front door. The bang! bang! bang! brought Carol's neighbor running to find out who was making all the noise. When she opened the door and saw only Tabby Cat, she knew something was wrong.

The neighbor followed as the little cat ran toward the open door of Carol's flat. It sat there staring back at her with a weird glint in its eyes, she thought afterward. When the neighbor looked inside the flat, she saw Carol lying motionless on the floor. She ran back to her home and dialled 999 for an ambulance.

Some hours later Carol opened her eyes in Wigan Infirmary. A nurse was standing by her bed with a very relieved look on her face. "Do you know that your life was saved by a cat?" she said.

When I visited Carol, she introduced me to Tabby Cat and showed me where her neighbor had found her, collapsed on the floor. Since that day, she assured me, Tabby Cat has been her constant companion. Without her pet, Carol would have died.

— ASSESSMENT —

Q1. Why do you think Tabby Cat jumped up and knocked at the neighbor's door?

a) The cat was bouncing around in the corridor and the neighbor heard it as knocking on the door.

b) The cat was frightened by Carol's sudden fall to the floor and was seeking attention.

c) Tabby Cat knew that Carol was in need of help and knocked at the neighbor's door to raise the alarm.

Q2. Do you believe that Tabby Cat saved Carol's life?

a) Carol's life was saved by the medical team at the hospital.

b) Only by accident. The frightened cat happened to alert the neighbor.

c) Tabby Cat purposely saved Carol's life by fetching the neighbor, who then called for an ambulance.

ZEUS: The Guardian Angel Dog

As guard dogs go, Great Danes are pretty good. None was much better than Zeus, 160 pounds of lean, mean burglar biter. With his owner Mary McCraken and her family, Zeus was like a determined warrior, and anyone unfortunate enough to enter on his patch without prior invitation was greeted with a very determined growl. With Zeus, what you saw was what you got – teeth!

The toughest dog in Texas

Mary lives with her family on the outskirts of Houston, Texas, in a spacious home standing in its own grounds. Over the years Zeus had established himself as the toughest guard dog around. He really looked the part, and friends of the family were always careful to book their visits by telephone first. Zeus had quite a reputation for frightening the pants off unsuspecting callers.

Then, in the autumn of 1995, one of Mary's close friends became seriously ill with a viral infection. After weeks of treatment in hospital, Jo Bronski was discharged into Mary's care. She had already prepared an apartment for Jo in a converted outbuilding some hundred yards away from the main house.

The first time Jo met Zeus, the Great Dane gave her a fearsome display of his teeth. But Jo didn't mind Zeus. He was a frightening sight when facing strangers, but she understood that he was just doing his duty. Zeus was everything a guard dog should be; in fact, he was everything two or three guard dogs should be.

Zeus runs for help

After about a year of living in Mary's care, Jo began to feel worse again. The viral infection had weakened her heart and, one afternoon in late summer, she suffered a stroke. The pain shot through her body and she could sense her life slipping away. "Help!" she cried, but her voice was too faint to carry to the house where Mary and the family were preparing dinner.

Zeus, who was patrolling the perimeter fence, heard Jo's weak little cry for assistance, and he came running. Bounding up to Jo, the Great Dane took one look and realized that help was needed. "Go get your mama, Zeus, go get Mary," Jo said to the dog. With one huge leap, Zeus was off.

Mary was surprised to see the dog as it ran into the

house. Normally Zeus preferred to stay outside on guard. Then she noticed that he seemed to be trying to get her attention: he was jumping from paw to paw and kept running to the door with an imploring look in his eyes. Mary thought there was trouble, perhaps a snake in the yard. Grabbing a brush, she followed Zeus out of the house. On the far side of the yard, she saw Jo slumped on the patio of her apartment. Zeus had run over and was standing by her side.

Mary called an ambulance and Jo was rushed into hospital, where she remained for over a week. When she returned to her apartment, Jo told Mary she was certain that Zeus had saved her life.

Zeus the protector

From that day onward, the Great Dane protected Jo. At various times during the day Zeus would go up to Jo's patio and, if she was sitting out in her rocking chair, put his huge head on her lap for a stroke. At night, just before bedtime, Zeus would jump up to Jo's window and nudge his nose against the glass. If Jo didn't respond with a wave or a call, the dog would go and fetch Mary.

It was really uncanny how Zeus, the terror of the neighborhood, had understood that Jo was ill and needed help. He gave the weak lady only love and affection. For hours on end the guard dog sat by Jo's side. He had become, she said, her very own guardian angel dog. To the day he died, Zeus continued to care for his friend Jo. She will never forget him and his compassion.

The McCraken family have two new guard dogs now, Zack and Zorro, but no matter how well they guard the home for Mary and her friend Jo, there will never be another like Zeus, the guardian angel dog.

— ASSESSMENT —

Q1. What do you think made Zeus such a good guard dog?
a) Zeus was a Great Dane. The mere sight of such a huge dog frightens off intruders.
b) The dog had been well trained to protect its owners' property.
c) Zeus was also the family pet. He was so good at guarding the McCrakens because they were his friends and he cared for them.

Q2. Why did Zeus change his attitude toward Jo when she became ill?
a) Zeus was guarding the McCrakens' property. When Jo stopped walking about, the dog had no reason to bark at her.
b) He thought perhaps she had become ill because he frightened her, and felt guilty.
c) Zeus knew that Jo was ill and did his best to protect her by fetching help. The dog was sensitive to Jo's needs.

DINKY: The Donkey That Loves Children

As a baby, Alexander Whelan-Archer was diagnosed as suffering from severe cerebral palsy, an illness that affects the central nervous system. He was also epileptic and had been born almost blind. The doctors said he would be lucky to live beyond the age of two. Refusing to believe that this baby boy would die so young, his adoptive mother Patsi devoted herself to caring for him. She had cared for children with special needs before, and thought that if she could just make little Alexander want to live, then he stood a chance.

Meeting Dinky

Over the months Patsi tried everything to give this boy the will to survive. She hung the main room in her home with Christmas lights, wore a silly tinsel wig, sang to him, danced, and generally did all she could think of to stimulate Alexander. Then she had an idea. Near her home in Sutton Coldfield in the English Midlands, there is the Elisabeth Svendsen Trust center where disabled youngsters are given free rides on donkeys. Patsi thought that Alexander might respond to meeting one of these friendly creatures.

Patsi telephoned the center's manager, Sue Brennan, and told her about Alexander, who was now two years old. They were both invited to visit the next day. That night as Patsi prepared Alexander for bed, she told him that she had ridden a donkey once, one distant sunny day on the beach at Blackpool. Now it would be his turn.

Inside the EST center, Sue Brennan introduced Patsi and Alexander to the staff. Carrying Alexander in her arms, Patsi followed the staff instructors to an indoor enclosure. There stood a donkey called Dinky, already saddled up. He was all white with twinkling eyes and pointed ears. Patsi lifted Alexander up and one of the staff placed his tiny hands on Dinky's nose. Dinky gave a little wriggle of his head and for a second Alexander pulled back with a frightened look on his face. Being nearly blind, Alexander could not see the donkey but his sense of touch was extra sensitive. The animal must have felt strange and hairy to him. But after a moment he let the staff put his hands back on that funny, friendly head. This time he stroked one of Dinky's long ears. Patsi, who was still holding Alexander in her arms, could feel the joy running through him. His whole fragile little body seemed to tremble with pleasure and a wonderful smile lit up his face.

Learning to ride

For the next six months Patsi took little Alexander to the EST center once a week. The boy loved every minute of it. The doctors at the hospital where he was born were astounded at how well and happy he was. Alexander was now all smiles and he tried his tiny best to control his limbs. The improvement in him so amazed the specialist in charge of Alexander's case that he asked if he could arrange an operation on the boy's eyes in an attempt to improve his vision.

Patsi will never forget the day she returned with her son to the EST center after his successful operation. Now little Alexander looked out at the world with beautiful clear green eyes. For the first time he could see his pal Dinky, and was able to ride without someone holding him.

Watching her child sitting on top of that donkey moved Patsi to tears. On the boy's face was a grin as wide as a mile. Alexander trotted round the arena laughing all the while as Dinky jogged him up and down. Patsi could see that despite all his terrible afflictions, her baby was, for once, gloriously happy.

The stars of the arena

Since that day Alexander has returned to the EST center at least once a week to see and ride his best friend Dinky the donkey. His treatment for cerebral palsy at a special school continues. This is helped along by the riding, which not only encourages the boy to use and control his muscles, but also brings great joy into his world.

By the age of six, Alexander had become one of the stars of the EST center. And much of his progress is thanks to a donkey called Dinky that just loves little children.

— ASSESSMENT —

Q1. Do you think Dinky helped Alexander to live?
a) The exercise and stimulation helped Alexander.
b) Dinky helped Alexander by giving the boy a lot of pleasure.
c) The donkey helped Alexander by making him feel wanted and loved. Dinky did this because he is a gentle and caring creature.

Q2. Do you think Dinky is Alexander's friend?
a) Dinky walks round the EST center like the good donkey he is, regardless of who is on his back.
b) Dinky recognizes and likes his regular visitors.
c) Dinky feels a special love for helpless little Alexander and would miss him if he didn't visit.

ITSY BIT: The Happy Hamster

Lois J. Barin is allergic to dogs, cats, horses, tree pollen, weeds, and hamsters. Whenever Lois comes into contact with any of these, she begins to sneeze, her eyes run, and breathing becomes difficult. Her consultant allergist has told her to have no contact with any of the above.

Lois is quite content to stay away from horses, dogs, cats, and of course weeds. But she simply can't resist hamsters. You see, hamsters make her happy.

From fishy stare to furry friend

It all began back in the year 1979. Lois knew she was allergic to many things, including most pets, but she just loves animals. She had to have a little friend to care for. Having tried befriending goldfish and getting nothing but a few bubbles and the odd fishy stare through the side of the tank, Lois reconsidered. Dogs and cats were out of the question. They would shed hair all over the house, reducing Lois to a coughing, sneezing wreck. What she needed was a much smaller creature, one that could be controlled within a small area. A friend suggested hamsters. As soon as Lois held one in her hand, she fell in love.

Her first furry pet was a long-haired hamster she called Bear. It wasn't really like a bear – much smaller! But it was very brave and would nibble even the biggest nut. Lois was captivated by this friendly little thing. Bear had so much personality and seemed to like entertaining Lois with funny tricks, running on its exercise wheel and hopping up and down the cage. To Lois, Bear seemed to be trying its little best to amuse, and in return she cared for the tiny creature.

This was the start of Lois's long love affair with hamsters. When she told her allergist, he was not amused, to put it mildly. However, it was too late. Lois was hooked on hamsters.

A hamster's degree

Over the next twelve years Lois looked after Bear and a succession of hamsters. She placed the cage near to the table holding her computer. As she worked away, writing her thesis for a Master's degree, her little pal would shuffle about, and whenever Lois looked at her pet, she felt relaxed. The sight of her funny furry friend going about its daily life brought joy into her heart. Often she would stop writing and feed her hamster pal a treat. The pleasure of watching it nibbling away cleared Lois's mind and filled her with peace and the strength to continue her demanding work.

Then, on the very day she was to present her Master's thesis to the board of examiners at Ohio State University, her latest hamster, a fluffy thing called the Grinch, died. The cage stood empty at the side of her desk; the little wheel that Grinch had loved to run upon was still. The silence in the room seemed to surround Lois. In that silence she remembered the happy hamster that she had loved and cared for. Then she began to sneeze.

Maybe it was the pollen in the air, maybe a nervous reaction to the sad loss of her pet. Whatever it was, Lois sniffled, coughed, and wheezed her way through the examination by the university professors. Despite this, she passed with flying colors.

Later that day, Lois went to see her allergist. When she told him about the death of the Grinch, far from sharing her sorrow, he seemed pleased. "No more animals!" he said, and made Lois promise, "No more hamsters." But it was a promise she was destined not to keep.

Just a little one

A few years later, Lois began studying for a Ph.D. She knew this would be hard work, made harder by the fact that she had no little furry friend to watch as she worked away each night on her computer. Still, if she wanted to achieve her goal, then work she must. The days were all right; she could see the squirrels and an occasional chipmunk climbing the trees outside her window from her desk. But the nights were lonely. There was an empty space where once the happy hamsters had played.

It was January, the cold winds blew through the deserted streets, and even the interior of Ohio State University seemed frozen. In the canteen Lois sat sipping a cup of tea with a group of her colleagues. She listened in horror as one lady told the group that her daughter's hamster had given birth again. "I hope the dog doesn't eat this one," she said.

"What!" Lois cried, outraged. "Your dog ate a baby hamster?"

"Why don't you take the hamster?" her friend said.

In a flash, Lois agreed. It might not please her allergist, but she couldn't let a lovely little furry baby get eaten by a great hungry hound.

That night she went round and collected it. The newborn hamster was no bigger than one of Lois's thumbs. As it nestled in the palm of her hand, she fell in love again.

Lois named her new pet Itsy Bit, because she was just an itsy-bitsy little thing. Back home she washed out the cage and cleaned everything so that it sparkled. Itsy Bit soon made herself at home and Lois placed the cage where it had stood before, next to her desk. As she sat, watching that tiny creature tunnelling into the wood chips and nibbling at the treats she had placed in the cage, she felt so much better. It was as if her home was complete now.

From then on, Lois would often stop working and gaze

at Itsy Bit as she played on her wheel or hopped around the cage making her little bed. Just watching this hamster brings happiness to Lois. She feels that they are both together, working hopefully, travelling forever forward toward some unseen goal. With Itsy Bit by her side, Lois knows that she has a friend on her long journey of self-discovery. And in this often difficult life the unselfish love of a true friend is something to be treasured above gold.

— ASSESSMENT —

Q1. Lois is allergic to furry creatures like hamsters, so why do you think she owns one?
a) Some people always feel they have to do the opposite of what they've been told. It is her way of living dangerously.
b) Hamsters are kept in cages, so she is not in contact with her pet all the time.
c) Of all animals, hamsters are the ones that make Lois feel happiest. What's a little allergy between friends?

Q2: What does Itsy Bit the hamster bring into Lois's life?
a) Lots of furry particles that tickle her nose and make her sneeze.
b) Entertainment and peace of mind, as she watches the creature's antics.
c) Unconditional love and constant company. As Lois works away on her computer, she can pause and see her true friend, little Itsy Bit, there by her side.

PET TEST No. 3: Is Your Pet a Feel-Good Pet?

I s your animal friend the kind of pet that makes people feel happy? Does it make them smile? If you're not sure, take this simple test. Follow the straightforward steps below, fill in the forms, and then complete the assessment at the end of the test to find out.

In Advance

1) Using the form at the end of these instructions, make a list of three friends and/or relations who are willing to take part in this test.

2) Explain to your volunteers that you are conducting a very simple experiment to see if your pet has what it takes to make people happy. All they need to do is agree to meet your pet at a time and place that best suit all concerned. Note the agreed dates and times on the form.

3) Explain to your pet that you want it to meet some of your friends. Talk gently and positively to your pet and think happy thoughts. Tell it what great fun this is going to be, and stroke it as you do so.

On the Day

4) Groom your pet. As you prepare it, continue talking gently and encourage it to be happy and at ease. The pet must look and feel its best for this test.

5) With your volunteer seated comfortably in an easy chair, introduce your pet. Just lead or carry your pet in and place it or tell it to sit close to your volunteer.

6) Watch carefully what happens now. Use the preprinted form to note the reaction of both pet and volunteer. At no time should you yourself become involved in the meeting between your pet and the volunteer. This is your pet's big chance to shine with its own charm.

7) After ten to fifteen minutes, collect your pet from the side of the volunteer. Now ask the volunteer the series of questions on the form and note the answers.

8) Repeat steps 4 to 7 with the other two volunteers.

9) Now complete the assessment form to discover whether your pet is a feel-good pet.

Volunteers

1)
Name ....
Address ....
....
....Post/Zip Code ....
Date and time of test:_____A.M./P.M._____/_____/_____

2)
Name ....
Address ....
....
....Post/Zip Code ....
Date and time of test:_____A.M./P.M._____/_____/_____

3)

Name ....

Address...

....

....Post/Zip Code ....

Date and time of test:_____A.M./P.M.____/____/____

Your Observations

Simply tick YES, NO, or MAYBE, whichever is the answer closest to your opinion, having watched your pet with the volunteers. NOTE: This form MUST be completed by you at the same time as the test.

	YES	NO	MAYBE
a) Pet seemed at ease with volunteer.			
No. 1	☐	☐	☐
No. 2	☐	☐	☐
No. 3	☐	☐	☐
b) Volunteer seemed very uneasy and tried to escape from pet.			
No. 1	☐	☐	☐
No. 2	☐	☐	☐
No. 3	☐	☐	☐
c) Did volunteer stroke your pet?			
No. 1	☐	☐	☐
No. 2	☐	☐	☐
No. 3	☐	☐	☐
d) Did volunteer smile?			
No. 1	☐	☐	☐

No. 2 ☐ ☐ ☐

No. 3 ☐ ☐ ☐

e) Did your pet show signs of enjoyment?

No. 1 ☐ ☐ ☐

No. 2 ☐ ☐ ☐

No. 3 ☐ ☐ ☐

Volunteers' Observations

At the end of each test, read your volunteer these statements and ask them to answer YES, NO, or MAYBE. Then tick their response in one of the three boxes.

	YES	NO	MAYBE

a) This animal made me happy. It is a feel-good pet.

No. 1 ☐ ☐ ☐

No. 2 ☐ ☐ ☐

No. 3 ☐ ☐ ☐

b) I felt at ease and enjoyed meeting this pet.

No. 1 ☐ ☐ ☐

No. 2 ☐ ☐ ☐

No. 3 ☐ ☐ ☐

c) I was a bit frightened of this pet.

No. 1 ☐ ☐ ☐

No. 2 ☐ ☐ ☐

No. 3 ☐ ☐ ☐

d) This pet is friendly and made me smile.

No. 1 ☐ ☐ ☐

No. 2 ☐ ☐ ☐

No. 3 ☐ ☐ ☐

e) AaaaaHHHhhhGGGGgggggggHHhhh!!!

No. 1 ☐ ☐ ☐

No. 2 ☐ ☐ ☐

No. 3 ☐ ☐ ☐

— Final Assessment —

Mark each of the three tests against the score sheet below. Then add the three sets of scores together to give you a joint total. Do this for both your observations and the volunteers' observations, then add both scores together to give you a final total. Now refer to the assessment to discover whether you have a pet that makes others feel good.

YOUR OBSERVATIONS

TOTAL FOR EACH VOLUNTEER:

	No. 1	No. 2	No. 3
a)	YES 3	NO 0	MAYBE 1
b)	YES 0	NO 3	MAYBE 1
c)	YES 3	NO 0	MAYBE 1
d)	YES 3	NO 0	MAYBE 1
e)	YES 3	NO 0	MAYBE 1

TOTAL SCORE

No. 1_____

No. 2_____

No. 3_____

JOINT TOTAL:_____

THE VOLUNTEER'S OBSERVATIONS

TOTAL FOR EACH VOLUNTEER:

	No. 1	No. 2	No. 3
a)	YES 3	NO 0	MAYBE 1
b)	YES 3	NO 3	MAYBE 1
c)	YES 0	NO 0	MAYBE 1
d)	YES 3	NO 0	MAYBE 1
e)	YES 0	NO 0	MAYBE 1

TOTAL SCORE
No. 1_____
No. 2_____
No. 3_____

JOINT TOTAL:_____

FINAL TOTAL:_____

— ASSESSMENT —

90–60 Congratulations! You are the owner of a real feel-good pet. Take it out to meet lots of people. They are bound to love this friendly creature.

59–30 Your pet has the potential to be a smilemaker but needs to meet more people and get used to strangers. Try asking your parents to talk to it a little each day – it may not make them smile but you can have a little giggle.

29–0 I knew someone would try this with a tarantula! Never mind, even if the volunteers failed to smile, I bet you had a good laugh.

TRIXIE: The Telepathic Rat Catcher

When Kym Grainger was an eight-year-old girl, her family moved into a rambling old house on the outskirts of Indianapolis, Indiana, in the heart of the American Midwest. The house had belonged to Kym's great-grandmother and was packed with family keepsakes. To little Kym it seemed like one big treasure chest. She loved exploring all the odd corners, especially the dark and spooky ones. Her favorite finds were the old paintings and pictures that seemed to hang in the strangest of places and on most of the walls.

The Grainger family had two huge German shepherd dogs called Prince and Trixie. Trixie was Kym's favorite and she often sneaked the dog a few treats from the dinner table. These family pets were real characters and always getting into mischief. There was no keeping them in; they could even escape from the fenced-in garden by great leaps. If Trixie, who was just a little smaller than Prince, couldn't make the jump in one, then the bigger dog would stand by the fence and let her leap up from his back. It was amazing to watch them. Then they'd both go tearing off round the neighborhood, having a right party together. These two dogs were inseparable pals; wherever you saw one bounding along, the other would arrive just seconds later.

Forgotten treasure

One day while Kym was exploring the buildings outside the old house, she saw the broken wooden doors to a rickety garage hanging half open. Damp and rot had split the timber and the paint had long since faded away, leaving a rust-brown shade. Kym had heard her father say that her great-grandmother used to own a big black Cadillac limousine. Perhaps it was still there. It would be the best playhouse ever.

Creaking open the first door, Kym peered inside. It was very dark and a stale, musty smell hung heavy in the air. Slowly her eyes adjusted to the gloom and she could see that the Cadillac was long gone. The place was full of packing cases, boxes, and old junk. To Kym it looked like a hoard of interesting objects. Braving the dank whiff of decay, she walked deeper into the darkness and pulled open a big leather trunk.

She was only a little disappointed to find busted tennis rackets, bent golf clubs, broken toys, and other rejected items. They all had potential as playthings. But the real treasures might be further in. She quickly set about searching through the rest of the cases, lifting out and trying on moth-eaten fox furs, worn-out shoes, torn coats, and unidentifiable rags. Apparently her great-grandmother never threw anything away.

Next, opening a battered old suitcase, Kym saw some photographs poking out of a ripped envelope. She couldn't wait to have a closer look. She pulled the whole case away from the old spring mattress it was resting on, and dragged it toward the dim light filtering in through a filthy window on the far wall. As she stared at the faded pictures, taken long before she was born, she wondered who those people were.

Red eyes and yellow teeth

Kym was totally wrapped up in her adventure of exploration. Suddenly she heard a sound like kittens crying.

Cats! she thought and turned toward the sound. It seemed to come from the back of the old mattress. She moved toward it, then froze with fear. Two red eyes shone in the darkness.

Kym's mouth went dry, and she could not look away. Gradually she made out the snarling face of a huge black rat. The beast's yellow teeth were bared and, as it glared at her, its pointed, scaly tail swished from side to side. Kym tried to scream but managed only a faint gasp.

Behind this nightmare creature was a nest of squirming baby rats. The big rat was guarding its young. Kym was sure this beast was about to kill her. Terror gripped her so that she was unable to move. Any second now, she thought, that rat is going to tear into me with its revolting teeth.

Then, with a sound like rushing wind, Trixie the dog whipped past her and snatched up the great rat in her jaws. The vile creature shrieked as the dog savaged it to death. Trixie threw the dead thing against the garage wall, walked up to the baby rats and looked at them contemptuously, and then came protectively to Kym's side.

Gently the big German shepherd pushed the trembling girl backward, out of the crumbling old garage and into the safety of the sunshine. Kym is quite certain that without Trixie she would have been badly bitten, maybe killed by the big black mother rat protecting its brood.

How did she know?

When Kym told her mother what had happened, she looked really surprised. "Trixie was playing with Prince and we wondered where she had run off to on her own. She never goes anywhere without Prince."

Kym held her mother tight and tears of relief ran down her cheeks. The terror of her experience had really shaken her. "How did Trixie know I needed help?" she asked.

Her mother had no idea. The dog had never been into the garage before, and running off without Prince was unheard of.

Today Kym is sure that Trixie had received some kind of telepathic message telling her that help was needed, fast. "How else," says Kym Grainger, "could the dog have arrived in a place it had never before been at exactly the time it was most needed?"

— ASSESSMENT —

Q1. How do you think Trixie knew that Kym was in danger?
a) Dogs have highly sensitive hearing. Perhaps Trixie heard Kym gasp in fear.
b) As Kym rooted about in the garage, the smell of the old junk wafted out through the door, and with it the smell of rats, which drew Trixie's attention.
c) Kym's mind sent out a call for help and Trixie picked this up telepathically.

Q2. Why do you think Trixie did not kill the baby rats?
a) The dog was saving them for later.
b) Trixie was more concerned with getting Kym out of the garage to safety.
c) The dog killed the big mother rat in response to a silent call from Kym's mind. With the baby rats no such call came.

CAPPY: The Earthquake Dog

In 1968 Linda Watt moved with her family to the town of Newhall in California. Her sons Shannon and Gregory were then ten and elven. The boys wanted a pet, so Linda took them to the local animal shelter. They picked out a beautiful long-haired German shepherd, and called her Gertrude.

Dogs by the dozen

The boys just loved Gertrude. Other dogs loved her too – lots of them. Soon Gertrude gave birth to puppies. There were twelve in all, six dogs and six bitches. They had the most wonderful coats: six were almost pure white and the others black and tan. The boys were sad when Linda explained that the family couldn't possibly keep them all, and the puppies were sold.

Before long, Gertrude was pregnant again. Linda had tried to keep her in, but Gertrude could jump right over the garden's seven-foot fence. In due course she gave birth to twelve more cute pups. Again Linda sold them to the townsfolk of Newhall. But this constant breeding had to stop! The town was filling up with cross-breed dogs.

The next time Gertrude came into season, Linda persuaded the local vet to lock her up in his secure kennels at the rear of his practice. That would keep Gertrude out of trouble, Linda thought.

She was wrong. The very first night Gertrude was locked in the kennels, she broke out. Not only that, but somehow she opened all the other dogs' cages and they ran free. Then Gertrude celebrated her escape by mating with General, the vet's huge pedigree German shepherd show dog. The vet was not amused.

Number 13

This time Gertrude gave birth to thirteen pups. The last one to be born was the runt of the litter. It was all wrinkly and weak, and hadn't got a hair on its body. The vet said it was certain to die, and Gertrude would not nurse it. But Linda wanted it to live. She used a glass eye-drop dispenser to feed the tiny creature milk and honey, water, and even some whiskey. The puppy was so small it could barely swallow, but it struggled and fought for its life. So hard did it try that the boys called it Captain Courageous, or Cappy for short.

Once again Linda sold all the healthy pups off, but Cappy, who was still very weak, became her own favorite little pet. Each day she would feed him and stroke his newly grown white coat. Cappy would push his tiny wet nose into Linda's hand and lick her fingers, just as he had done as a day-old pup.

To keep Cappy warm, Linda let him sleep on an electrically heated pad used by her sons to ease aching muscles after playing sports. The puppy loved this, it was so nice and warm. Then one day, when Cappy's teeth were growing, he bit into the electric cable. The shock caused him to pee and that made things much worse – he was almost electrocuted to death.

From that day on Cappy would never go near a bed or any other item of furniture. He obviously thought they would give him an electric shock.

Earthquake

On February 2nd, 1972, at 4:49 A.M. Western U.S. time, Linda woke from a deep sleep to find Cappy on the bed, standing on her stomach. The dog was growling and crying in a pitiful way, pulling and tugging at Linda's nightgown as if trying to drag her out of bed.

Linda was shocked. What, she wondered, could Cappy want at this time in the morning? He always slept downstairs and hated beds, so there was obviously something wrong. Then the dog jumped off the bed and ran out through the door, heading toward her sons' room.

It was then that she heard a booming crack which she recognized as being the start of an earthquake. As fast as she could, Linda dashed into the boys' bedroom and got them out of bed. Quickly they ran downstairs out of the house and into the middle of the garden.

There were more loud underground explosions. Suddenly, amid flashes and sparks, everywhere was plunged into total darkness as the electricity lines came crashing down. From where the Watt family stood on the lawn, they could see, in the moonlight, the house shaking like a tree in a high wind. The ground was heaving and trembling beneath their feet.

Cappy was there with them, making sure they were all right. He was barking with excitement, jumping up and licking the boys' faces. They were safe, and he had helped save them.

Right to the minute

For five days Linda, her sons, and all the townsfolk were trapped within the valley because the roads leading in and out had collapsed. Many homes were damaged beyond repair. The earthquake had measured 6.9 on the Richter scale and their town was just four miles from the epicentre.

During the days they were trapped, the area suffered numerous aftershocks. Cappy seemed able to predict these just as he had the main one. From sitting quite still, he would quickly stand up, turning round and round on the spot, looking hard at the ground. Each time he did this, within ten minutes, a minor earthquake followed. Because so many houses were in ruins, other families temporarily shared the Watts' home. They all saw Cappy behaving this way. He became known as Cappy, the earthquake dog, and everyone in the area knew of his ability to predict quakes.

One night, about three days after the initial shock, Cappy started his by now familiar routine of jumping up and running round on the spot. Everyone watched the dog and looked at the clock. Seven minutes passed, no quake; eight minutes passed, nothing; nine minutes, total silence – the tension was terrible. Just as the second hand swept to mark ten minutes, one woman who could stand it no longer shouted 'SHAKE, SHAKE!' at the top of her voice. She nearly collapsed as the earth began to tremble underneath her. Cappy had been right again.

A debt repaid

Cappy repeated his earthquake-warning dance many, many times throughout his life and he was never wrong once. If ever there was an impending earth tremor over 3 points on the Richter scale, Cappy would dance.

Linda Watt is quite certain that the German shepherd saved her and her sons' lives that dreadful night in 1972. When she examined the house after the quake, all the wardrobes in the bedrooms had fallen over and smashed into the beds. If her boys had been in there asleep, they and she might easily have been killed. Little Captain

Courageous had more than repaid Linda and her sons for saving his life all those years before, when he had been the last puppy, the runt of the litter.

— ASSESSMENT —

Q1. How do you think Cappy knew there was going to be an earthquake?

a) Cappy smelled a gas issuing from the earth's crust as it began to shift before the big quake.

b) Dogs have very sensitive ears; Cappy heard the rumbles before Linda did.

c) Dogs have a sixth sense for danger and perhaps Cappy was made aware of the forthcoming earthquake by mystical means.

Q2. Why did Cappy go upstairs to raise the alarm rather than run out of the house?

a) Perhaps the doors to the house were all locked and Cappy was trying to wake Linda so she would open them and let him out.

b) Cappy knew that Linda fed and cared for him so he needed her to survive.

c) The dog had developed a bond of love with Linda and her family. They had raised him from puppyhood when his own mother had rejected him. So Cappy wanted to save his friends.

JOSIE: The Parrot That Nursed His "Momma"

Tina Marie Smith lives in Tampa, Florida, with her husband Jimmy and a collection of birds. The owner of four cockatiels, in August 1991 Tina was asked to give a home to an unwanted Amazon parrot. She at once agreed.

A bird in a gilded cage

When the bird arrived, Tina was surprised to see its extremely ornate cage. There were wire spires at each corner and an amazing dome at the top. Inside, the perches were cut from highly polished dowelling. It looked like the kind of cage any design-conscious parrot would love.

The parrot was called Josie and he had a magnificent bright-yellow blaze on his head, like a sunshine cap. His neck feathers were brilliant red and his long green wings were sprinkled with blue. Sitting quietly in that strange cage with his hooked beak half open, he looked a real character. Tina lifted him out to examine him, and placed him on a soft cushion.

Josie instantly fell into a deep sleep. The bird's long wings spread out wide and his head turned to one side as his tiny eyes closed. It was as if he had collapsed with relief on being released from a prison. Tina took a closer look at his fancy cage and almost cried. Locked in there, the bird had obviously been unable to rest properly. The perches were far too shiny and thick for the bird to grip; one of his claws was badly damaged from trying to get a foothold. Two perches were far too close to the top of the cage for Josie, who was a big bird. His right eye was injured, too. And the glittering silver water dish was almost out of reach. This was no friendly home for a parrot to be happy in; this was an instrument of torture.

As the parrot slept, he kept making little cooing noises of contentment. Tina knew then that this was a very special bird. He was her little friend and she would look after him. "Come on, baby," she said. "You'll be fine now. Momma's here." The parrot made a tiny cooing noise as if in response. Tina was in love.

Gently Tina stroked Josie's marvellous plumage and spoke softly to the sleeping bird, whispering words of encouragement. How sad, she thought, that such a beautiful living thing should be injured through the thoughtless actions of supposedly more intelligent beings.

A new home for Josie

That very afternoon Jimmy built Josie a new, parrot-friendly cage. This one had perches that the bird could actually sit on, a water dish and feeding bowl within easy reach, and, best of all, a door that would be opened every day. Tina nursed the poorly parrot for days, feeding him bits of fresh fruit. He soon became a healthy bird and was happy hopping round Tina's house. Often he would hop into the utility room and hide behind the clothes dryer, where he could be heard flapping his wings.

Tina hand-fed Josie and stroked him. On warm summer evenings, he would join her on the porch outside her house. The parrot would just sit quietly beside his friend and take in the fresh air. Those were happy days for Tina and Josie.

Amazon parrots are noted talkers, they have a knack for picking up odd words and phrases, but for years Josie did no more than impersonate next door's horse. He really had the sound off and could make the most realistic whinnying noise that Tina had ever heard outside a stable.

Josie's first word

Early in 1997 Tina became ill. For months she had been complaining of headaches and finally, one bleak January morning, she collapsed. Jimmy was away at work and she was alone in the house – alone except for her feathered friends. Her head was spinning as an agonizing pain shot like a thousand volts of electricity into her brain.

As Tina lay on the couch where she had fallen, she felt a fluttering at the side of her cheek. Turning her head, she saw Josie. He had jumped out of his cage and hopped over to the couch where she was lying. His wing was outstretched stroking her face. As Tina looked in amazement, she heard the very strangest thing. Josie opened his beak and said, "Momma."

The shock cleared Tina's pain right away. The bird had spoken to her, stroked her aching head and comforted her. Years before when the parrot had first come to live with her, and she had nursed it back to health, she had said to the bird, "You'll be fine now. Momma's here." She thought Josie must have remembered and, seeing his friend sick and injured, had come to nurse her, just as she had nursed him when he had been a poorly parrot.

A practical joker

Since then Josie has really started talking. He calls out to Tina, "Open the door, Momma!" when he wants a hop around the room or a wing-flapping session behind the clothes dryer. He still impersonates the horse and has learned a new trick, to bark like next door's dog. This is very confusing for Tina, who has been worried that the dog might get in and attack her birds. Time and time again she has run in expecting to see the hound in her living room, only to discover Josie woofing away on his perch. The strangest thing is that he seems to know it's a joke. He always ends the barking with a giggle that sounds just like Tina laughing.

Tina's headaches come and go. When they hit, she just goes to the couch and lies still. And, weird as it may seem, Josie knows when she is in pain and hops up beside her. The parrot has become Tina's special little nurse and she is his surrogate momma.

— ASSESSMENT —

Q1. Why do you think Josie stroked Tina's head with his wing?
a) He was flapping his wings to get attention.
b) He remembered being stroked by Tina and was just copying her.
c) He saw that his friend was ill and went to comfort her.

Q2. Do you think that Josie really is playing a joke on Tina when he barks like a dog?
a) Parrots repeat noises at random and people like to read meaning into them. Josie would repeat them even if Tina was not in the house.
b) Josie has linked the two sounds of barking and laughing and knows they always get him attention.
c) Josie knows that Tina is worried about next door's dog and imitates the sound of its bark to fool her. The parrot then imitates Tina's laugh when she comes into the room, to show that this is a good joke.

SNOWBALL: The Prescription Pet

Patsy Taylor lives in Arkansas, USA, in a neat little apartment on the outskirts of the town of Searcy. She has many friends in the town and her home is often full of visitors. But Patsy lives alone, and this was becoming a problem because she suffers from epilepsy. It could be extremely dangerous if she had an epileptic fit while, for example, cooking on a hot stove. She might fall against the cooker and burn herself or set the house on fire.

Such worries were starting to make Patsy depressed. Yet she did not want to leave her apartment and move in with friends. She loved her home, and had taken pride and pleasure in furnishing it. Everyone said how neat and tidy she kept it.

Snowball lands

Then one of Patsy's friends had to move away from the

area to take up a new job in another city. The lady, Mrs. Woods, didn't know what to do with her pet spitz dog. The apartment she was moving to was far too small for pets and anyway the lease prohibited the keeping of anything bigger than a goldfish. Dogs were definitely not allowed. She was telling Patsy about her problem when they had an idea: Patsy could take the dog. It was well trained and would be company for her. That very afternoon Mrs. Woods brought the pet round.

The dog was a snuggly bundle of fur and she was called Snowball. Patsy fell in love with the cuddly pet straight away and bought lots of little treats for her, doggie chews and biscuits, to make her feel welcome and wanted. They soon became great friends and Snowball followed Patsy everywhere.

A dog with superpowers

It was about a week after Snowball first came to live with Patsy that a very strange thing happened. Patsy was sitting quietly in her most comfortable fireside chair reading a book. Then, when she decided to go and make a cup of tea, Snowball stopped her. The dog jumped up and pushed Patsy back into her seat just as she started to rise.

She tried again but Snowball would not let her out of the chair. The dog placed its big floppy paws on Patsy's waist and pushed her back. Thinking this was very odd indeed, Patsy decided to sit still and wait till the dog moved, but it didn't. Suddenly Patsy began to feel the onset of one of her awful epileptic fits. Thank goodness she was in a chair! Knowing what she had to do to prevent herself from being injured, Patsy relaxed as best she could and let the attack take its course.

When she opened her eyes again, Snowball was sitting by her feet. Patsy stood up and walked to the bathroom. Snowball didn't interfere. Having freshened up, Patsy went to make that cup of tea she had tried to make before Snowball had stopped her.

As she put the kettle on the open gas burner, she thought of what might have happened if she had had an attack while the kettle was on. She could have fallen against the flames and caused a real fire. In her mind she thought that Snowball had sensed the onset of her epileptic attack before she had, and that the dog, knowing the danger, had prevented her from getting out of the chair where she had been safe.

Patsy had been an epileptic all her life. She knew that the attacks were unpredictable. One moment she would be fine, the next faint and falling to the floor. It seemed incredible to her that a dog could sense such an attack before she did – impossible, even.

The doctor is baffled

Two days later it happened again. Patsy was doing the week's washing and had just begun loading all the clothes into the spin dryer when she felt Snowball pulling at her skirt. The dog would not let go; with all its might it pulled and pulled at Patsy's skirt until she followed her pet into the living room. There Snowball forcibly pushed her into the fireside chair. Within three minutes Patsy had another epileptic fit. The dog had somehow foreseen this and had acted to protect her new owner.

The next week Patsy Taylor was due to see her doctor for her regular monthly check-up. When she told her doctor about Snowball's amazing ability to sense the onset of her epileptic attacks and warn her in advance, the doctor refused to believe her. This was, he said, just her imagination. Well, Patsy knew it wasn't. She invited the doctor round to her apartment to meet her pet.

Soon afterward, therefore, when the doctor was in the area of Patsy's home, he decided to call in. He had been there only a short time when he saw the spitz jump up on Patsy's lap. Snowball pushed her nose hard into Patsy's chest, forcing her deeper back into her chair. The doctor stared in amazement as, less than two minutes later, Patsy had an epileptic fit. The dog had warned her of it and had protected her. Had she been standing up, Patsy would have fallen to the floor and could have injured herself.

The prescription pet

About three months later the management of the apartment complex where Patsy had her home found out that she was keeping a dog. This was against the rules. They gave her a week to get rid of Snowball. The very idea broke Patsy's heart.

In desperation she went to see her doctor. When Patsy told him that the housing manager had ordered her to get rid of Snowball, he was most displeased. "Right, Patsy," he said, writing something down on his pad, "take this to your housing man and tell him this is a medical prescription."

When Patsy read what he had written, she smiled. It said: "One spitz dog name of Snowball to be used as resident protective companion at all times." The doctor had prescribed her own pet as treatment.

When Patsy showed the housing-complex manager the doctor's order, he agreed that since it was a medical requirement, she could keep her pet.

To this day Patsy remains safe and protected by her dog. They are the best of friends and Patsy's life is much happier now she knows that Snowball is there to look after her.

— ASSESSMENT —

Q1. Do you think Snowball knew that Patsy was going to have an epileptic fit?
a) The dog was probably just jumping up to play. The fact that Patsy had an epileptic fit afterward is a coincidence.
b) Snowball could smell a chemical change in Patsy's body just before an epileptic fit.
c) Snowball sensed that Patsy needed protection, so she jumped up and stopped her from moving.

Q2. Why do you think the doctor prescribed Snowball as a medical aid to Patsy?
a) He disliked unnecessary house rules and was glad to help his patient to keep her dog.
b) He had noticed that having a dog kept Patsy in good spirits, and this improved her health.
c) The doctor believed that Snowball could tell when Patsy was about to have an epileptic fit, and that the dog would help to protect her.

SMOKY: The Reincarnating Cat

Marilyn Johnson loved horse riding. It was the one thing guaranteed to clear her mind of the working week's problems. She kept her horse, a dapple-grey named Stony, on a Western-style ranch in Reno, Nevada, USA. Each Saturday and Sunday Marilyn would drive out to the stables and ride with friends into the wild beauty of the Sierra Nevada mountains. Riding Stony, her spirited thoroughbred, was a challenge that made Marilyn happy.

A chance meeting

One autumn afternoon, while she was grooming Stony, Marilyn saw some kittens coming out from an empty stable. They appeared to be no more than a few weeks old. She stood for a moment just looking at the tiny creatures and was captivated by one black kitten. She thought its eyes sparkled with personality. Although its mother was living almost wild on the ranch, this kitten seemed calm and friendly.

Marilyn was reminded of her childhood pet cat Powderpuff. She had cried for days when that puss had died, and she had never had the heart to buy another. She felt no cat could replace Powderpuff. But this little kitten seemed so kindly and, in an odd way, familiar, so she asked the ranch owners if she could buy it from them. They just laughed and told her to take it. The kittens' mother was always producing litters and the ranch had more cats than it needed.

Picking her new little friend up, Marilyn carried it back to the car. Looking closely at the cat, she noticed again its mysterious eyes. They reminded her of the swirling mists of an early spring morning before the sun chases them away. Marilyn named her pet Smoky.

A strange resemblance

Each night when Marilyn came home from work, Smoky would be waiting. She used to sit near the front door so she could see when her owner's car arrived. As soon as Marilyn entered the house, she would scoop Smoky up in her arms and listen with joy to her pet's purr of love. The sound eased away the stress of Marilyn's working day. At night Smoky would sleep curled up comfortably at the foot of her bed. She seemed to know Marilyn's routine and was always there waiting for her at bedtime.

Over the years Smoky became more and more attuned to Marilyn. Often she would look at the cat and think just how much it reminded her of her childhood pet Powderpuff. The likeness was really uncanny. Whenever she was feeling sad, Smoky would be there to comfort her with a little meow as she rubbed her soft little body up against Marilyn's legs.

A life companion

Then Marilyn's world turned almost upside down. First she and her husband divorced and she left Nevada, moving to California. Smoky and Stony came along, of course, and it was their love that helped keep Marilyn sane. Then, over the next few years, both her mother and father passed away. But Smoky was there, her constant companion and friend. Life was tough for Marilyn and, at times, hardly seemed worth living. One dark night, when everything became too much for her, she sat alone in her room just crying and crying. Smoky jumped up on the bed and stared at her with those mysterious shining eyes, as if the cat understood that her friend needed some help.

Marilyn cried and the tears trickled down her face, wetting her cheeks. As she lay there lost in sorrow, the little cat cuddled up by the side of her neck and softly began to brush those teardrops away with its tiny paws.

From that day on Marilyn felt she had a friend whom she could trust with her innermost feelings. Often she would lift Smoky up and tell her all that was troubling her. The bond of love with her cat helped Marilyn through the next eighteen years. When Smoky died, it left a big gap in Marilyn's life.

A mismatch

Marilyn wanted another cat to be her friend, so she went to the local animal-rescue unit and asked whether they had any kittens. There she saw a lovely little black pussy with white paws and bib. She took it home and tried to befriend it, but this cat was too independent. It wasn't a bit like Smoky.

After a few years of trying to attune herself to the new cat, Marilyn confided in a friend. She told her all about Smoky and the great love the cat had brought her, and that her new pet was too self-contained. Marilyn's friend told her that cats pick the people they want to love and live with, not the other way round.

Marilyn thought about this and it seemed to be true. Certainly the new cat was not her best friend the way Smoky had been. While she would always care for the cat and give it a good home, there was no close bond of love between them. Marilyn began to miss Smoky more than ever.

A flood victim

During the winter of 1996, the rains half flooded California. Everywhere there was mud and puddles. One day Marilyn took her horse to a local vet. As she led Stony out of the trailer, a little girl came up to her and said, "There's a kitten over there that's been hurt in the floods."

Marilyn tied Stony's reins to the box and followed the child to see whether she could help. What she saw made her think she was dreaming, for the kitten was the absolute image of Smoky.

Dropping down on her knees, Marilyn picked up the tiny creature. It was wet through and its fur was all muddy. Gently stroking the cat, she observed the way it responded. She was not disappointed: the little kitten purred with love just as Smoky used to. She had found a friend.

Taking the kitten home, Marilyn gave her a good wash. Her markings were the same as Smoky's, and when she walked into her bedroom, the little kitten followed. Marilyn called her Smoky II and is certain that this cat is the reincarnation of Smoky. She believes that her old friend, seeing she was sad without her, has come back in a new body to help her all over again.

Smoky II sits in exactly the same places as Smoky I. She also waits by the front door for Marilyn to come home. In fact, the kitten looked up at Marilyn as soon as she called out "Smoky!", just as if she knew her name. Even stranger are Smoky II's eyes. They are like the swirling mists you sometimes see on an early spring morning, before the sun chases them away.

— ASSESSMENT —

Q1. Why do you think Marilyn thought that Smoky was like her childhood pet Powderpuff?
a) She was in need of a friend, and that made her imagine the likeness.
b) Smoky had many of Powderpuff's physical characteristics.
c) Smoky was in fact the reincarnation of Powderpuff.

Q2. What made Smoky the cat stroke away Marilyn's tears?
a) Cats like a little salt, and tears taste salty.
b) People in highly emotional states can imagine lots of things like this.
c) Knowing that Marilyn was sad, Smoky was comforting her.

SASHA: The Protector

In the city of Ottawa, Canada, there lives a lady whose pet dog has become her protector. For many years Reggie Lajeunesse and Sasha, a little Lhasa apso with a long coat and sniffy nose, have been best pals. All Reggie's friends and family love Sasha, and the dog in turn has always had a special liking for Reggie's younger brother Jack. Jack often visits and always brings a special treat for Sasha, a bone from the butcher's shop or a pack of her favorite dog biscuits. Sasha even seems to know when Jack is going to call and sits by the front door in happy anticipation.

Turning against an old friend

One day about six years ago, Reggie became quite seriously ill. The doctor diagnosed food poisoning. For days she could not eat. Gradually she began to weaken. Concerned for his sister's health, Jack drove over to see if he could help in any way. When he arrived he found a very different Sasha from the one he was used to meeting.

As Jack walked through Reggie's front door, he saw the little dog standing at the doorway of his sister's bedroom. "Hello, Sasha!" he said and threw her a biscuit he had brought as a treat. The dog ignored the titbit, bared her teeth, and growled. Jack wondered what he had done wrong. When he tried to go into Reggie's bedroom, he found out that Sasha wasn't going to let him. The little Lhasa apso was guarding her friend and would not let Jack in, biscuit or no biscuit. Jack thought she was ready to bite him.

After two failed attempts to get past Sasha, Jack called out to his sister. Confined to her bed, Reggie was unaware that her pal had appointed herself her protector. She could hear the growling and shouting and wondered what was going on, but she never thought that Sasha would have turned into a guard dog.

Still weak from her illness, Reggie struggled to the bedroom door and picked little Sasha up. Back in bed, she set her pet on the covers and held her collar. Each time Jack got a little too close, the dog snarled and showed her teeth in a quite frightening way. There was no doubt in Reggie's mind, nor in Jack's, that the dog was on guard.

Back to normal

Some weeks later, when Reggie had returned to good health, Jack called round to see his sister. There, waiting at the front door, was little Sasha. The dog had seemingly known that Jack was coming and had been sitting waiting for over half an hour. When Sasha saw Reggie's brother she ran up and licked his hand, hoping to receive her customary treat. Sure enough, Jack gave her a dog biscuit he had bought specially for Sasha from the pet shop. It was as if the incident at the bedroom door had never happened.

Reggie is sure that Sasha knew she was very ill and had been protecting her. The Lhasa apso was only small compared to Jack, but he says there was no way he would have dared to go any closer than he did. Sasha would have protected her friend from anyone during the period of her illness. After all, if Jack with his biscuit treats couldn't get close, who could?

— ASSESSMENT —

Q1. Do you think Sasha can tell when Jack is coming to visit?

a) Dogs don't foretell the future. If Sasha happens to sit by the door when he arrives, Jack likes to think she has been waiting for him.

b) Sasha can sense Reggie's anticipation, and perhaps recognizes the name Jack and associates it with treats.

c) Sasha is telepathically aware of Jack's approach.

Q2. Why do you think Sasha tried to stop Jack from entering Reggie's bedroom?

a) The dog may have been in a bad mood, probably caused by receiving no attention because her owner was in bed. Certainly Jack posed no threat to Reggie so the guard theory is a nonstarter.

b) Dogs can sense when things are not quite normal and Sasha was probably upset by Reggie's unusual behavior.

c) The dog sensed that Reggie was ill and was protecting her from anyone and everything that might get near.

CHARLIE: The Raccoon That Brought Love

Don Bouldrey, a computer service engineer living in Alabama, near the Gulf of Mexico, found a baby raccoon one fine day in May 1994. Don had been planting his garden when he noticed that Sunny, one of his two pet dogs, was nosing around a spot near the fence at the far end of his plot. Wondering what the dog had found, he walked over and saw, lying on the ground at the foot of an old oak tree, a tiny raccoon that Sunny had pulled from its den. The little creature couldn't have been more that a few weeks old, and looked all but dead.

Carol, Don's wife, helped him clean the baby raccoon. It was covered in dirt, and flies had laid eggs on its body in expectation of the creature's death. Carefully they washed away the filth and fed it lukewarm milk with added vitamins. Although it was female, Don named the raccoon Charlie. The creature's total helplessness touched something deep in his soul. As he gently stroked her head, he spoke softly, telling the tiny wild thing that she had to live. Charlie's parents had probably died and she had been left alone in her den. She could not have fended for herself – her little eyes had not yet opened, she was so young. But Don was determined to save Charlie.

A beard has its uses

Hour after hour Don and Carol nursed Charlie, dripping milk formula from an eyedropper into the raccoon's mouth. Then Don had an idea that would ensure the little thing wouldn't choke. He lifted the animal onto his chest and dribbled some of the milk formula on his beard. Charlie nuzzled up and licked the feed off Don's whiskers, much as she would have done with her own mother. So when Charlie opened her shiny black eyes, the first thing she saw was Don smiling down at her, with milk dripping off his bushy beard.

Over the next few days, Charlie began to get stronger. Holding her in his hands, Don pressed Charlie close to his chest and whispered words of encouragement. Perhaps the tiny raccoon understood; Don thinks she did, for as days turned to weeks, Charlie began to walk. At first not very far, just a few faltering steps across Carol's lounge carpet, but she was going to live. At night she slept in box beside Don and Carol's bed. She still enjoyed cuddling up to Don and would curl her little raccoon fingers around his beard, tugging at it as though in search of the milk she used to drink there.

Within one month Charlie was almost fully fit and exploring the garden. She soon mastered the art of escaping through the dogs' special flap-door, but she always returned. Carol was quite certain that the raccoon knew them as friends. Charlie would come when called and take food from their hands, just like a pet. However, both Don and Carol realized that raccoons belong in the wild. They hoped that one day soon, when Charlie was strong enough, she would return to her fellow creatures.

In the meantime they loved having this adorable little house guest. Her coat was rather special: she had silver rings on her otherwise jet-black fur with a wonderful silver tip to her long bushy tail. Charlie was the most beautiful raccoon they had ever seen. All their friends thought she was lovely, especially when they saw her sitting in a corner sucking on her thumb. She was the cutest little creature, and seemed so contented, as though she had adopted Don and Carol as her parents.

The comforter

After a couple of months Charlie had begun to venture out beyond the garden and would often be seen climbing in the trees nearby. The time was approaching when she would find a friendly raccoon and disappear into the wild where she really belonged. Don and Carol accepted that it was natural for her to do this, and felt pleased that they had helped this happy little creature to live.

Don's work servicing computers requires a great deal of intense concentration. One day he came home with a terrible headache. His brain seemed to throb, and blinding flashes of light streaked in front of his tightly closed eyes. Throwing himself face down on the couch, Don thought

he was going to die. He had taken two aspirin tablets but the pain was getting worse, not better.

Suddenly he felt a furry thing pushing underneath his hands and snuggling up to his face. It was Charlie. She wriggled and pushed against Don's nose and her tiny clawed paws stroked his neck. Then the raccoon jumped up and started to howl and scream as if calling for help. Carol came over to comfort Don, and was surprised to see Charlie push herself under his head and poke her thumb into his mouth. It was as if Charlie was saying, "Suck this thumb, it will calm you down." Strangely, through the terrible pain of his headache, Don remembers doing just that, and feeling the relief flood through him. The little raccoon had brought him her comforting thumb and Don had sucked it, just like a baby.

Never sit on an ants' nest

In Alabama there are fire ants – ants that sting and inject a
poison that burns painfully. Unknown to Don, there was a
nest of these ants at the far end of his garden. One of Don's
two dogs, Leo, a golden retriever, found this nest when he
sat down. They stung his bottom severely.

The sound of Leo howling in pain brought Carol and
Don running from the house. To their surprise Charlie followed. As Carol held the squirming Leo, Don squirted the
dog's bottom with a jet of water from the hosepipe, in an
attempt to shift the ants that were crawling all over him.
This didn't work, so Carol got a metal comb and began
combing them out of Leo's long fur. As she was doing this,
Charlie jumped up on the dog's back and started picking
ants out from within the fur, just like a monkey. Don and
Carol were amazed at Charlie's cleverness and her will-
ingess to help, as if she were tuned in to the whole family
and wanted to play her part.

A savage deed

One day Charlie went missing. Don and Carol looked
everywhere but she was not to be found. They hoped she
had found herself a raccoon friend and returned to the wild,
but Don wanted to be sure she wasn't just lost. Over the
weeks Charlie had taken to exploring further and further
afield and would often hide up in the eaves of the house,
coming for food when called. He looked and called, but no
Charlie. As twilight turned to night, he searched through
the trees, just where he had first found Charlie only a few
months before. Already he missed his friend and hoped
that, wherever she was, her life would be a happy one.

It was two days later that Don discovered the tragic fate

of his friend Charlie. As he searched through a nearby pecan orchard, he saw a black plastic bag. Suddenly his mind raced; he ran over and ripped it open. There, dead and still, lay little Charlie. A bullet had torn into her back, ripping away part of her rear left leg. But the shot had not killed Charlie outright, the plastic of the bag bore testament to this. Don saw the little rips made by her claws as the dying animal had struggled to escape from within its folds. Too late he had come, too late this time to save his friend who had died trapped inside that black shroud.

It was as if a thunderbolt had struck Don. He stood trembling with rage as tears poured down his cheeks. Who had done this? Who could kill such a glorious and harmless creature? Don was determined to find out.

That night he went round to the house next to the pecan orchard and asked the woman who answered the door if she knew anything about the dead raccoon in the plastic bag.

"Oh," she said, "I love pets and thought it had come round to be my friend, but it climbed into the eaves of my house and wouldn't come down. So I telephoned some animal lovers I know and they said it must have rabies, so I just poked it out with a stick and shot it. I used over twenty bullets, I'm not much of a shot."

The horror of that admission took a while to sink into Don's mind. How could someone who professes to love animals do such a thing? Twenty shots! Charlie must have been terrified. And then to shove her poor injured body still alive into a plastic bag and throw it into a field to die! The tears burned his cheeks as he choked back his feelings. The words to describe this callous woman dried in his mouth and would not be spoken.

A lasting memory

That evening they laid Charlie to rest. At the foot of the old oak, just where Don had found her those few months before, he dug a grave and placed her lifeless body in the dark-red, dusty soil. They marked Charlie's grave with a simple stone, but the gentle love and compassion she had brought into their lives has left a deeper mark. For there is a place within their hearts that will forever belong to Charlie, the little raccoon that brought them love.

— ASSESSMENT —

Q1. Do you think Charlie was special?

a) To Don and Carol she was. But she probably only did what raccoons do.

b) Her trying to help Don and the dog when they were in pain shows that she was a good and clever creature.

c) Yes, she understood that Don wanted her to live and gave him love in return.

Q2. What did Don and Carol actually get from caring for Charlie?

a) One thing they did get was trouble with the neighbors. Don will probably never talk to that woman again.

b) They learned a great deal about raccoons and their habits.

c) They learned that even a wild animal can bring love and compassion into people's lives.

THE FEELINGS OF ANIMALS: What the Scientists Say

Coming across the stories in this book, and many other anecdotes like them, I began to wonder how well we really understand animals, and what is known to science about their feelings. To me it is obvious that Grumbles, my bulldog, jumps for joy when I reach for her lead. She knows that the lead means she is going for a walk and this makes her happy. If I have to go out and leave her alone, Grumbles actually cries. I have often heard her, as I close the front door, making a soft mewing noise as if to say, "Don't go without me!" When I return, she throws herself from left to right in excitement, so hard she sometimes turns full circle. Yet happiness and sadness as we conceive of them are human emotions. Can we ever really know what our pets feel?

Animals are not like human beings

Animals do not perceive the world in the same way we do. Some of their senses are more acute than ours, and others less so. For example, a dog has a very sensitive nose and uses its sense of smell a great deal in checking out its surroundings. A dog's picture of the world is therefore hard for us to imagine. The feelings of a fish can hardly even be guessed at.

All we can say for sure about animals is what we observe

of their behavior. Some scientists stress that it is more accurate to say "The bulldog is wagging its tail" than "The bulldog is happy". If you ever accidentally tread on a cat's tail, the sudden pain will trigger fight-or-flight chemicals in the cat's brain, and you will see the behavior of a cross cat. Whether it feels exactly the way you do when you're angry is another question. But you might as well treat it with respect.

The attribution of human feelings to animals is called anthropomorphism. In science, this is avoided, because it may lead to misunderstanding. When we go out and leave the dog alone, it seems reasonable to translate "The dog is making a whimpering noise" into "The dog is unhappy", but that does not necessarily mean that it is forming a picture of a lonely evening stretching ahead of it, with nothing to do except play a game of patience.

Over 120 years ago, the famous English naturalist Charles Darwin, the author of *The Origin of Species*, suggested that animals might have feelings similar to humans. The subject has been debated ever since. We still do not know enough about the physiological basis for emotions even in humans.

Experiments on animals

Some animals are used for experiments in laboratory conditions. Many of those carrying out tests on living creatures argue that the suffering caused to animals in experiments and drug tests is justifiable if it leads to discoveries of new drugs, surgical techniques, or other ways of curing sick people. They point out that if a new drug causes birth defects, it is better to find out by using it first on mice rather than on people.

Those who oppose animal testing say that it is always wrong deliberately to cause suffering, that the work of doing so is brutalizing, or that the results of animal tests do not always apply to humans, because they are physically different. They point out that testing of cosmetics on animals – by squirting the ingredients into their eyes, or by painting their little furry faces – is no longer standard practice since the public began to object to it. And no one has died yet of mascara overdose or lipstick rash.

The conditions in which laboratory animals are kept have often been criticized. It is easier for laboratory workers to subject the animals to harsh tests if they have not given them names and played with them. And they know the creatures are likely to be killed at the end of the experiment anyway. People who support animal testing like to tell themselves that since animals cannot feel exactly as we do, they do not feel at all. But, having read the stories in this book, can you really believe that?

Emotional responses in animals

All my life I have had a pet. I even used to feed the spiders in my grandparents' cellar when I was little more than a baby. I used to stick the food into the vast cobwebs that my tiny friends had spun on the dusty window frames. I like to think my actions made them happy, though at the time I didn't realize that spiders eat flies, not half-chewed bits of candy bars.

A wildlife biologist who was brave enough to go up and offer a piece of meat to a big black bear – don't try this even at the zoo! – was rewarded by a squealing sound that he thought was an adult version of the sound made by bear cubs being nursed by their mother. He decided that this squealing is the sound bears make when they are happy. They feel content and they communicate this.

Visiting a zoo, Charles Darwin once saw the rhinoceros let out of its winter pen for the first time that year. "Such a sight has seldom been seen," he wrote, "as the rhinoceros kicking and rearing out of joy." He was sure he was watching a happy animal.

A frightened animal is also easy to recognize. My bulldog trusts me, but no sooner do we set foot in the vet's clinic than Grumbles crouches down on the floor and tries to hide under my feet. Charles Darwin was among the first to describe the signs of fear in animals. He listed these as: open mouth, eyes rolling from side to side, heartbeat increased, hair stands on end, teeth chatter, muscles tremble, animal cowers down or freezes still. Not unlike you or me when faced with a terrifying situation. This reaction is associated with certain chemicals (such as epinephrine, also called adrenaline) being produced in the animal's body.

Sorrow is not so easy to determine in animals. I can still remember finding Tweety, my little budgie, dead on the floor of its cage when I was just a boy of seven. My father put Tweety in a little box and we buried it in our back garden. I cried as my dad said a few brief words over that little pal of mine. Do animals weep too?

A world expert on gorillas has written that she once saw a gorilla sobbing. A four-year-old she called Coco had watched as its family was killed by the hunters that captured it. They locked little Coco in a cramped wooden cage. When Dian Fossey released the young gorilla, she watched in amazement as it stared in wonder at the trees and the mountains; then Coco burst into tears, crying and sobbing like a little child.

Similar behavior has been reported of elephants. And closer to home, many owners of poodles say that their pets have wept tears on being left at home as they go out. We can't dismiss this as crocodile tears!

Most pet owners will say they love their animal friends. Many believe that this love is returned by their pet. I was recently stroking Grumbles and telling her what a really beautiful girl she was. Now it may sound soft but I do love my bulldog and I think she knows this. Anyway, as I tickled behind her floppy old ears, she pushed her face right up to me and gave me a big wet lick with her tongue. For a moment I felt all happy inside: I am sure she was telling me, in the only way she could, that she loved me too.

Of course, the kind of love that human beings feel for each other is different from the love animals feel. Because we can think and talk and make long-term plans, our emotions are more complex. Scientists would say that animal love is based on kinship and survival.

Human beings are animals too

We people are ourselves animals, of the species *Homo sapiens*. We think ourselves to be the wisest creatures on this planet we call Earth. Yet we do not always behave toward either our fellow human beings or other living things as though we are wise. Over the last few hundred years our actions toward the creatures of the wild have wiped out many species, and endangered the existence of thousands more. In the U.S.A. the buffalo, or bison, that once ran in their hundreds of thousands over the wide plains now survive only in protected areas, and the huge condor that soared between California's mountains is on the verge of extinction. In Africa no elephant or rhinoceros is safe from poachers. As the dominant species on planet Earth we have, in a relatively short space of time, destroyed the natural habitats of countless thousands of wild animals and killed millions, sometimes just for "fun".

Imagine if creatures from outer space decided to invade Earth and hunt human beings for sport. We would have no difficulty deciding that they were wrong. Yet we have inflicted almost exactly the same kind of treatment as that depicted in alien-invasion movies upon innocent members of the animal kingdom.

What do you think?

In this book there are many stories about animals that have helped to make human beings feel better. No matter what the scientists think about the reason that these creatures behave as they do, what we should all be asking ourselves is, What do I think? If, like me, you think that animals have emotions, that they do feel joy and sorrow, fear and pain, then surely you could never deliberately hurt one of God's innocent creatures. I know I couldn't – what would Grumbles think of me if I did?

FINAL
ASSESSMENT

Each story in this book has an assessment section at the end of it. You should now total all your answers and refer to the final assessment chart below to discover what you think about the idea that animals make you feel better.

Mostly As

Your scientific mind is selecting the most rational options. You may even be skeptical about the true nature of the behavior of the animals in these stories. Although you may agree that something positive happened to the people featured in this book, you doubt that the animals played the part ascribed to them. You prefer the idea that individuals make themselves feel better through their love of pets to the notion that animals intentionally set out to make people feel better.

Mostly Bs

You agree that some animals form a bond with the human beings that care for them, but you do not fully believe that it is a bond of love as we know it. You are wary of attributing complex human emotions to members of other species. You are a very careful person and your choice of the B answers shows that you think things through. Your understanding of the nature of animals is not just scientific, you also feel love for them. You'd like to think that animals want to be our friends and make us feel better, but you will accept them as they are.

Mostly Cs

You have no doubt that animals want to make people feel better. By selecting mostly C answers, you have taken the choice of your heart. Inside you just know that our pet friends love us to bits, and don't you love them too? Your generous and loving nature will make you the ideal owner of many pets throughout your life. They will respond to your care with happiness and affection, for you have trust and hope within you. Animals can sense this and they are going to cuddle you to pieces. Grumbles sends a big lick.